SPIN-OUTS

Creating businesses from university intellectual property

By Graham Richards

HARRIMAN HOUSE LTD

3A Penns Road
Petersfield
Hampshire
GU32 2EW
GREAT BRITAIN

Tel: +44 (0)1730 233870
Fax: +44 (0)1730 233880
Email: enquiries@harriman-house.com
Website: www.harriman-house.com

First published in Great Britain in 2009

Copyright © Harriman House Ltd

The right of Graham Richards to be identified as the author has been asserted
in accordance with the Copyright, Design and Patents Act 1988.

ISBN 1-905641-98-2
ISBN13 978-1-905641-98-7

British Library Cataloguing in Publication Data
A CIP catalogue record for this book can be obtained from the British Library.

Printed in the UK by the MPG Books Group

Contents

To Margaret Thatcher,

who made much of this possible.

Preface

Spin-out companies from university science departments are very fashionable, important and much encouraged by governments. The new high-tech companies offer the hope of keeping Western economies viable at a time when much manufacturing is being outsourced to developing countries. At the same time they are the best possible means by which those same developing countries can move away from a mere reliance on cheap labour and develop their own sophisticated industrial enterprises. They can also be a means of sustaining university finances, an idea reinforced recently in the UK by the Lambert Report.

The aim of this book is to provide help to those tempted to follow the route of building a company based on the research conducted in university laboratories. The role of technology transfer offices and the technicalities of creating a spin-out company are covered, but the bulk of the text is devoted to the case study of Oxford Molecular, the company spun-out from the University of Oxford in 1989. The author was the scientific founder of Oxford Molecular, and this led to his involvement in a wide range of spin-out companies. This experience enables him to tell exactly how things are in practice, and to recount the high spots and the failures he encountered.

Recently retired from Oxford, where he was head of the University Chemistry Department, the biggest chemistry department in the Western world, the author was involved in 1988 in the founding of the University of Oxford's technology transfer company, Isis Innovation Ltd, of which he was a director for some 20 years. He was also a director of Catalyst Biomedica Ltd, which for a time was the technology transfer organisation charged with exploiting the intellectual property generated through research funded by The Wellcome Trust, the world's second biggest charity (after the Gates Foundation). He was chairman of IP2IPO Group Plc, the company resulting from a deal he did with Beeson Gregory Ltd in 2001 in order to fund a new chemistry research laboratory, and now itself the publicly quoted IP Group Plc of which he is senior non-executive director.

Graham Richards' range of experience, which he has gained as a long-term senior academic scientist and through involvement with a number of spin-out companies, makes him the ideal guide on how to spin out a company from a university. He knows what it is really like in practice, including the inevitable difficulties, and he can offer useful guidance on where this increasingly important sector will head in the future. This book will be of interest to universities, academia and business readers alike.

1

Introduction

The role of University science departments is to teach and to do research. This has always been the case and remains their most important function. Only relatively recently has the additional expectation emerged whereby the intellectual property they generate should be exploited for the public benefit. This is possible without compromising the traditional values, which nonetheless must remain at the forefront. Exploitation can be achieved by one of two mechanisms. Either the research can be licensed to outside companies who will pay royalties, or alternatively new companies, spin-outs, can be created.

Spin-Out Companies

Although licence income can be very significant, it tends to come in slowly and only the very rare example generates huge sums of money. This has in the past been more true of novel drugs than any other area. The returns are more likely to come quickly from the founding of a spin-out company, although this is more complex and time-consuming.

The University of Oxford has an outstanding record in the area of spin-out companies and I have been fortunate to be closely involved in many aspects of this activity. After the university set up its technology transfer company Isis Innovation, the first spin-out company came from my research group, Oxford Molecular Ltd. This paved the way in particular for companies derived from the Chemistry Department, which has played a unique role. This single department has contributed more than £80 million to the central university – £40 million in un-earmarked cash from sales of shares in quoted companies, £20 million represented in unrealised holdings in quoted spin-outs from the department and a further £20 million represented by the fair value of its equity in companies which are still private.

Oxford Molecular

Oxford Molecular is the company which we will take as a model, not necessarily of how it should be done, but as a case study of a very typical story. It was founded by me and my former researcher Tony Marchington in 1989. We took the company from a £350,000 start-up to a public company with an initial public offering (IPO) in 1994. It grew to have a capitalised value of £450 million following several takeovers, notably in the USA. At its height the company employed nearly 500 people, half of them in America where we operated five sites. We made mistakes and in the year 2000 the company was sold for some £70 million. Oxford Molecular yielded almost £10 million for the university.

Following how the story of this particular company panned out should be helpful to any academic embarking on this route and also give any incoming management some idea of what they are likely to face.

IP Group Plc

Oxford Molecular was a pioneering UK example of a university spin-out company in which the university itself held shares. The model was repeated numerous times in Oxford and elsewhere so that there has grown up a commercial sector of companies whose role is to create, foster and develop university spin-outs. Pre-eminent in this field is IP Group Plc. This grew out of an original arrangement which I made on behalf of the Chemistry Department of Oxford with a London-based company then known as Beeson Gregory Ltd. The agreement was that for an upfront sum they would receive half of the university's equity in any spin-outs from the Chemistry Department for a fixed period of time. That deal proved to be outstandingly successful for all the parties involved. It was developed into a separate company which now has similar arrangements with 10 UK universities and also operates in continental Europe. The way in which this company has grown, and its role in generating new companies, is also a tale which has lessons for academic entrepreneurs and for university technology transfer organisations which have been set up to accelerate company formation.

Before going into these case studies it will be helpful to give a brief account of how the story of university spin-outs has developed and to discuss the nature of technology transfer including the technicalities of setting up a spin-out company.

2

A Brief History Of Spin-Outs

University spin-out companies are not new. Probably the first was the Oxford University Press, founded in 1478 and still going strong. Interestingly it has never actually been spun-out and remains technically a part of the University of Oxford, with no shareholders and no obligation to pay corporation tax.

Despite that early start, Oxford came late to the business of creating companies based upon the research being conducted as part of the normal functioning of a seat of learning. Universities are about teaching and research. Spin-out companies are a by-product, even though they may be important for a country's financial health and major contributors to university funds.

Oxford Instruments was founded in 1959 by Martin and Audrey Wood but the university played no part in the formation of the company, whose origins were in the Physics Department. In that department at the time there was a need for magnets, and with this being the staple product of the company the university became the first customer.

The modern history of high technology companies is firmly focussed on the United States, and in particular Silicon Valley in California and the Route 128 area of Massachusetts, with the influence of Stanford University and Massachusetts Institute of Technology being a vital component.

The California Story

The San Francisco Bay area was a major site for US Navy work, including the large Navy aviation research centre at Moffett Field. This led to a growth in aerospace related companies, but the civilian high technology enterprises had their origins at Stanford University. Dean of Engineering Frederick Terman encouraged students to stay in the

Palo Alto area by finding venture capital for them, with William Hewlett and David Packard setting up Hewlett-Packard in 1939.

In the 1950s Stanford Research Park was created, providing low-cost industrial buildings for technical companies. Once again the influence of one individual was crucial in turning the region into Silicon Valley. William Shockley, who had quit Bell Labs in 1953, moved to Mountain View to create the Shockley Semiconductor Laboratory as part of Beckman Instruments. Shockley's difficulties with his colleagues led to a distinguished group of them, often dubbed as "the traitorous eight", resigning. The group includes now legendary names in the world of hi-tech business: Julius Blank, Victor Grinich, Jean Hoerni, Eugene Kleiner, Jay Last, Gordon Moore, Robert Noyce and Sheldon Roberts. With funding from the eastern US company Fairchild Camera and Instrument, they started Fairchild Semiconductors to make silicon transistors.

During the 1960s several of the original founders left Fairchild to form their own companies: the "Fairchildren". Massively successful examples included Intel, founded by Robert Noyce and Gordon Moore, and over the years this pattern repeated itself several times, so that there grew to be a critical mass which attracted the all-important venture capital groups and support services, such as specialist lawyers, to the region.

The presence of Stanford University and the campuses of the University of California in the region were critical factors in providing novel science and high quality people, but these companies cannot really be called spin-outs. The universities often benefited from the generosity of alumni who had created significant wealth through their entrepreneurial activity, but the universities were not directly involved in the creation of the companies and did not take founders' equity.

The Massachusetts Story

The same is true of the similar development of high technology, especially electronics companies, on the 65 mile highway, Route 128, around Boston. The Massachusetts Institute of Technology, along with Harvard and the other fine universities of the region, provided much of the intellectual input, and the US government, through the Department of Defence and the National Science Foundation, provided the funding. This was more evident on the US east coast than in California. In addition, the big successful companies such as Digital Equipment Corporation and Raytheon provided capital and, more importantly, acted as customers for the start-up companies.

As in California the benefits to the universities were indirect, albeit substantial. The companies were start-ups with the involvement of individual entrepreneurial academics as founders or technical advisors. The universities themselves did not place as much emphasis on starting companies as on licensing the technology they owned to the companies.

The Bayh-Dole Act

In 1980 the United States became concerned about declining productivity and rising competition from Japan. As a response Congress passed the Bayh-Dole Act, which enabled universities to patent federally funded research on a large scale. Universities were offered the opportunity to licence campus-based inventions to private companies in exchange for royalties. In the years following, Congress passed a number of additional laws to encourage university-industry links, notably generous tax breaks for corporations willing to invest in academic research. The Act permits the university to pursue ownership of an invention in preference to the government who had sponsored the research.

The impact of this legislation can scarcely be overstated. There was a ten-fold increase in patents generated and cumulative increases in industry funding for universities, rising to an annual $2 billion by the turn of the millennium. There are those who are unhappy about the Bayh-Dole provisions since in a sense giving private firms the rights to inventions generated at public expense means that the public has to pay twice for the same invention – once through taxes to support the research that yielded the invention, and then again through higher monopoly prices and restricted supply when the invention reaches the market.

The legislation does contain safeguards such as a "march in" provision enabling the federal government to terminate an exclusive licence if the licensee fails to take effective steps to bring the invention into practical application within three years. A royalty-free licence is also included to enable the government to use the technology at any time.

What is quite certain is the fact that the Bayh-Dole Act produced a massive increase in the amount of academic research being commercialised in the USA, more in terms of licensing than in the creation of spin-out companies.

The British Story

Virtually nothing happened in the UK until Mrs Thatcher shook up the system. The much repeated truism that Britain is good at invention, but poor at exploitation, is based on a long history of innovative science and woeful commercial success. In the 19th century Perkin produced the first synthetic dye, mauveine, and even started to manufacture it commercially. The country had a unique lead, but by 1914 when it was necessary to send an army to France, the only source of khaki dye for the uniforms was Deutsche Farbe and some of the British Expeditionary

Force went to war in navy blue uniforms dyed with woad, the natural dye favoured by the ancient Britons.

The BBC started television broadcasts in 1938, some ten years before a television service began in the USA, but by the end of the 1960s there were no British companies making TV sets. Computing is often traced back to Babbage, but the first modern electronic computer was built at Bletchley as part of the Enigma code cracking project by Tommy Flowers, based on the theoretical work of Alan Turing. In the early 1960s possibly the best electronic computers in the world were built by the UK Ferranti company. My first experience of computing was with the wonderful Ferranti Mercury in 1961. By the 1970s the industry had disappeared overseas.

The modern era was much influenced by the Second World War. In the dark days of 1941 when Britain stood alone after the fall of France, the USA came to the aid of the old country by providing 50 ships to help make up for convoy losses in the Atlantic. The deal was known as "lend-lease", since at its heart was the provision of permanent leases on bases in the West Indies to the Americans. Less widely known is the fact that in the small print of the agreement between Churchill and Roosevelt, the UK agreed not to patent three strategic British inventions: radar, the jet engine and penicillin. All were potentially vital to the war effort and only the USA had the industrial power to exploit these technologies. They helped the allies to win the war, but at huge financial loss to post-war Britain.

That fact was not lost on the post-war Atlee British government which in 1948 set up the National Research and Development Corporation (the NRDC). This nationalised body was created to commercialise innovations resulting from publicly funded research, at government research centres and universities, with research support from the state-funded research councils. Amongst their successes were the cephalosporin antibiotics, developed in the same Oxford laboratories which had exploited penicillin, magnetic resonance imaging and Interferon. The NRDC became the British Technology Group (BTG) following a merger with the National Enterprise Board, and was privatised in 1992.

In its days as a state monopoly, the NRDC, despite some striking successes, was essentially risk averse and not subject to normal commercial pressures. They turned down the hovercraft and, most notoriously, decided that monoclonal antibodies were not worth patenting. This they did under the reign of Margaret Thatcher who had great sensitivity to commercialisation (she was an Oxford-trained chemist). Indeed she had been responsible for another crucial innovation – changing the taxation rules to permit and encourage venture capital, which did not exist in the UK before 1982.

In 1987 she again took a seminal decision to hand over the ownership of intellectual property derived from government funding to the universities in which the IP had been generated, provided they set up a mechanism to encourage exploitation, or as it has become known "technology transfer". This crucial step set the stage for the flowering of spin-outs in the UK.

3

Technology Transfer

Technology transfer is a current buzz phrase. It relates to the creation of wealth from the intellectual capital generated in universities. In some respects it is a new label for things which have gone on for a very long time, even at a university as venerable and academic as Oxford.

At the time of the founding of Oxford Instruments, which became the world's leading supplier of super-conducting magnets, the attitude of Oxford was dominated not by potential wealth creation, but by fear of liability. This near paranoia was not totally without foundation. In the 1920s, a university professor named Owen developed and patented a machine to extract sugar from beet, which was licenced to an Italian food company. Unfortunately the device was fraudulent and the university was sued for what at the time was a very significant sum. Legend has it that Owen ended up in jail where he reputedly swindled the prison warders out of their savings.

The result of this disaster was to make the university totally risk averse and not interested in its intellectual property, which to be really safe it gave to the individual researchers.

If one attended presentations from the NRDC in the early 1980s, they presented a very positive view. A simple graph showing the income to the NRDC starting in 1947 indicated a steady increase and impressive return. They appeared to be a rare exception amongst nationalised industries in being efficient and, what is more, very profitable. In fact the massive income relied almost solely on two sets of patents – the pyrethroid insecticides from the Rothampsted Laboratories, and the cephalosporin antibiotics discovered in Oxford's Pathology Department.

The latter example is also illustrative of the effects of the university policy on the ownership of intellectual property. The profits on the cephalosporins went in part to the university researchers, but the university itself got nothing directly. Indirectly one of the researchers, Sir Edward Abraham, used much of his own return to set up trusts which have subsequently been very generous benefactors to university projects.

University Ownership Of IP

After the Thatcher revolution of 1987, some universities made contracts with BTG to exploit their newly-owned IP. Other universities set up their own organisations: in the Oxford case a wholly owned subsidiary company, Isis Innovation Ltd, was established and charged with exploiting the university's IP. For this to make any real sense it is obviously essential for the university to own the intellectual property and currently, unlike in the past, the university owns all the IP generated in its departments. It also pays patent and legal costs, investing well over £1 million each year. This clear-cut situation did not come about over night though, as the academic community needed to be convinced that this arrangement was to their advantage.

It is not easy to convince an intelligent academic of the proposition with logic such as: "at the moment you own the IP related to your research, but in future we, the university, will own it and you will be better off." This is because it is not obvious that having the legal and patent costs covered, and a generous reward system in place, is beneficial to the academic. If they just take the IP and file their own patents it often happens that as soon as the patent costs rise to thousands of pounds they let the patent lapse, which is the worst of all possible worlds. The world at large is now informed of the idea or invention and it is not protected. Of course in some rare instances individuals have become rich in this way, but in general that is not the case.

Hence this transfer of the ownership of the IP to the university was done in stages over about a 15-year period. Firstly, all work by those appointed after 1985 was drawn in, and then all work carried out after a set date, and then finally all work done at any time. At the same time, as well as being absolved from the expense of owning IP, very generous arrangements were established in terms of the revenues to go to the individual academics. These arrangements have seemed satisfactory enough so that only a couple of academics out of several thousand have questioned the equity of the scheme. This absolute clarity of the ownership of the IP is crucial to its exploitation and technology transfer.

It is essential for Isis Innovation Ltd to be absolutely clear, when dealing with third parties, about the ownership of the intellectual property. It would be disastrous if, subsequent to striking a deal with a major company, someone came along and challenged the ownership. This clarity is achieved by having a separate entity within the university administration responsible for clarifying and agreeing all contracts and grants obtained by academics before any IP is assigned to the separate company Isis Innovation Ltd. The internal organisation, the Research Services Office (RSO), vets all agreements and protects academics, who are eager to accept funding, from signing away rights. It is all too easy for a researcher to accept funding for a post-doctoral research assistant but in so doing sign away their rights not only to work legitimately claimed by the backer, but also to all similar work for all time. The RSO sees all grant applications, consultancy agreements and the like, using in-house lawyers where necessary. In this way the team in Isis Innovation can be sure that they are on firm ground when negotiating licensing deals or acting for the university in setting up a spin-out company.

Income Sharing

In terms of licensing, the Oxford model was developed to encourage researchers to seek protection of their work prior to publication. The major portion of initial financial returns from a licence go to the researcher, with a sliding scale as shown in Table 1. It is also wise for the department of the academic concerned to benefit from any major financial gain, as this encourages heads of departments to support the entrepreneurial activities of their younger colleagues.

Royalty sharing

• Isis Innovation pays all patent costs: £1.4m in the year to March 2007

• Isis recovers patent costs from royalties

• Isis retains 30% of royalties

• The net revenue is transferred to the university and distributed

Total net revenue	Researchers personally	University general fund	Department funds
to £50k	87.5%	12.5%	0
to £500k	45%	30%	25%
over £500k	22.5%	40%	37.5%

Table 1: Dispersal of initial investments

In the case of spin-out companies there has to be an all-important three way meeting to agree on the split of equity. This involves the interested parties: first, whoever puts up the funding, the venture capitalist or more likely business angels; second, Isis Innovation acting for the university which owns the IP; and third, the researcher or researchers without whom nothing can happen. The result of this negotiation, where each party may need independent legal advice, is a division of the shares in the new company. A typical split might be 40% to the backers, with 10% kept back for management of the newco, particularly the CEO, 25% to the university and 25% to the researchers. At this seed stage, however, there are many variables and there is no strict rule about this, only that the totals must add up to 100%. The intellectual property is invariably licensed to the new company rather than assigned, so that in the event of the company failing the IP returns to the university.

The Innovation Society

When Isis was founded in 1988 many of these aspects – ownership of intellectual property, licensing rules and equity splits – were not clear. Nor was the university's commitment to the idea of commercialising work generated in its departments. The university hired Dr James Hiddleston as its first managing director of Isis, a man who had appropriate industrial experience but who was unfamiliar with the peculiarities and politics of universities, especially the esoteric Oxford. He was given very little support and for several years was forced to run the organisation with essentially just himself and a secretary. The only significant source of financial support came from setting up a sort of club, the Oxford Innovation Society. I can claim credit for the idea of the society since I suggested it following success which I had in getting industrial support for protein structure studies involving crystallography, nuclear magnetic resonance and chemistry at the Interdisciplinary Research Centre (IRC) in Molecular Sciences. I managed to raise some £600,000 in the form of annual subscriptions from companies who received an inside track on the research output by way of preprints and exclusive meetings. James, however, took the notion and built a very successful Innovation Society that has been maintained for nearly 20 years.

Almost 50 companies pay an annual fee of a few thousand pounds to be members. In return they get three dinner meetings in an Oxford College, usually Trinity College, and a 30-day exclusive view of licensing opportunities. In fact, it is the dinner aspect which appears to be the more highly valued part. Each dinner has been sponsored by one of the member organisations and is preceded by a couple of talks: one from a university researcher who has something potentially commercial to show, and one business talk normally from the sponsor. The whole evening is a marvellous opportunity for networking and has produced a wealth of collaborations and research support. In the early days the membership was dominated by industrial companies such as pharmaceutical giants. Over the years the balance has swung and the membership changed as companies dropped out, either due to mergers or because they felt that they had built their networks and no longer needed the society. Increasingly the participants are banks, patent agents and support services, which is good news since it shows that these bodies are developing relations with Isis and the university. Table 2 lists the current (2008) membership.

Oxford Innovation Society – Members

Abel & Imray	Manches
Arlington Securities plc	MEPC – Milton Park
Barclays Bank plc	Lonza AG
Barker Brettell	Mills & Reeve
Blake Lapthorn Tarlo Lyons	NESTA
Boult Wade Tennant	Oxford Instruments plc
BP International Ltd	PA Consulting
Camitri Technologies	Parkgrove Limited
Canon Europe Ltd	Perlegen Sciences
CMS Cameron McKenna LLP	Pfizer Ltd
Consensus Business Group	Procter & Gamble
De La Rue	Roche Diagnostics GmbH
Elkington & Fife LLP	SABMiller plc
Frank B Dehn & Co	SEEDA
Genzyme	Siemens Magnet Technology Ltd
Harrison Goddard Foote	Sumitomo Chemical Co Ltd
Hitachi Chemicals	Syngenta
J.A. Kemp & Co	TATA Chemicals
James Cowper	Triteq Ltd
L.E.A. Investments	Wilmer Hale

Table 2: Membership of the Oxford Innovation Society, 2008

Great credit must go to Dr Hiddleston for driving the Innovation Society forward, but his limited resources meant that in the early 1990s scant progress was made in creating companies, as you will see from the information in Table 3, which shows details of Oxford spin-out companies up to 1998.

Year	Company	Capital	Equity	Main Business
1959	Oxford Instruments	£92m	–	Scientific Instruments
1977	Oxford Lasers	–	–	Lasers
1988	Oxford GlycoSciences	£102m*	Yes	Glycobiology
1989	Oxford Molecular	£53m*	Yes	Drug design
1992	Oxford Asymmetry	£316m*	Yes	Chemistry
1994	PowderJect	£542m*	Yes	Drug delivery
1996	Oxford BioMedica	£68m	Yes	Gene therapy
1997	Oxagen	–	Yes	Genetics
1997	Oxford Gene Technology	–	Yes	Gene chips
Total	–	£1,173m	–	–

*Quoted valuations at 20/10/03 or at sale of company

Table 3: Oxford spin-outs pre-1998

This list does include some significant successes, but it is very short and in reality Isis only played a direct role in perhaps three of these.

The Post-1998 Story

In 1998 James was succeeded as managing director by Dr Tim Cook. Tim had a number of advantages. He had studied Physics at Oxford and has an Oxford doctorate in cryogenics, thus combining pure science and engineering. He had worked for Oxford Instruments, and hence had been influenced by its founder Martin Wood, as well as being managing director of some small technology based start-up companies. Most significantly he had been the founding managing director of Oxford Asymmetry, the spin-out from the Chemistry Department based on the research of Steve Davies. The enormous success of that company permitted Tim to become a business angel, founding Oxford Semiconductors.

This background gave him the confidence, on being offered the job, to ask for six months to study what was needed and then to ask the university for proper support. He got it, and a revolution began. Whereas James received backing to the tune of £40,000 from the university, Tim persuaded the central finance department to provide investment of a few hundred thousand pounds a year for his first couple of years, and then £1 million per year for a guaranteed five year plan, to cover patenting and legal costs. The effect has been dramatic, as Table 4 indicates.

1998

Company	Main Business
Opsys Ltd	Displays. Now subsidiary of Cambridge Display Technology Ltd.
Synaptica Ltd	Neurogenerative diseases. Ceased trading.
Prolysis Ltd www.prolysis.co.uk	Antibiotics
Celoxica Ltd www.celoxica.com	Accelerated computing
Sense Proteomic Ltd (Now Procognia Ltd)	Protein pharmaceuticals

1999

Company	Main Business
AuC Sensing Ltd www.auc.co.uk	Sensors
Avidex Ltd www.medigene.de	T-cell receptors. Acquired by Medigene AG.
Dash Technologies Ltd	Merged with Celoxica Ltd
Oxonica Ltd www.oxonica.com	Nanomaterials
Oxon Therapeutics Ltd www.oxfordbiomedica.com	Vaccines. Acquired by Oxford Biomedica Plc

2000

Company	Main Business
Mindweavers Ltd www.mindweavers.co.uk	Learning systems
Mirada Solutions Ltd	Imaging. Now part of Siemens Medical Imaging.
Oxford BioSensors Ltd www.oxford-biosensors.com	Diagnostics
Oxford BioSignals Ltd www.oxford-biosignals.com	Signal interpretation
PharmaDM www.pharmadm.com	Data mining
Third Phase Ltd www.cmedltd.com	Electronic data capture, now Cmed Technology Ltd

2001

Company	Main Business
Inhibox Ltd www.inhibox.com	Computational drug discovery
Natural Motion Ltd www.naturalmotion.com	Animation
Novarc Ltd	Press tooling. Liquidated
Oxford Ancestors Ltd www.oxfordancestors.com	Genealogy

2001 continued

Company	Main Business
Oxford ArchDigital Ltd	Digital archaeology
OxLoc Ltd www.oxloc.com	GPS/GSM tracking
The Oxford Bee Company	Pollination. Ceased trading

2002

Company	Main Business
Oxford Risk www.oxfordrisk.com	Risk analysis
BioAnalab Ltd www.bioanalab.com	Pharma testing
Oxford Immunotec Ltd www.oxfordimmunotec.com	TB diagnostics
Oxitec Ltd www.oxitec.com	Insect pest control
Glycoform Ltd www.glycoform.co.uk	Glycochemistry
Zyentia Ltd	Protein misfolding
Spinox Ltd www.oxfordbiomaterials.com	Biomaterials. Now Oxford Biomaterials Ltd
Minervation Ltd www.minervation.com	Evidence-based mental health
Pharminox Ltd www.pharminox.com	Anticancer drugs

2003

Company	Main Business
OCSI Ltd www.ocsi.co.uk	Social inclusion consulting
Riotech Pharmaceuticals Ltd	Hepatitis drug delivery
ReOx Ltd	Drug discovery
VastOx Ltd www.summitplc.com	Drug discovery and toxicology. Now Summit Plc

2004

Company	Main Business
EKB Technology Ltd www.ekbtechnology.com	Bioprocess engineering
Surface Therapeutics Ltd www.serentis.com	Dermatological drugs. Acquired by Serentis Inc
G-Nostics Ltd	Anti-smoking test
Oxford Medical Diagnostics	Breath analysis. Merged with Avacta Ltd

2005

Company	Main Business
Oxford Catalysis Ltd www.oxfordcatalysts.com	Catalysts. Now Oxford Catalysts Plc
Oxford Nanolabs Ltd	Nanopore technology. Now Oxford Nanopore Ltd
RF Sensors Ltd www.oxfordrfsensors.com	Sensors
Celleron Ltd	Oncology drugs

2006

Company	Main Business
Cytox Ltd	Diagnostics
Oxtox Ltd	Drug testing
Oxford Advanced Surfaces Ltd www.oxfordsurfaces.com	Surface chemistry. Now Oxford Advances Surfaces Plc
Aurox Ltd	Microscopy
Particle Therapeutics Ltd www.particletherapeutics.com	Drug delivery
Oxford Medistress	Blood tests
TdeltaS Ltd	Performance foods

2007

Company	Main Business
Crysallin Ltd	Nanostructured materials
Oxford Biodynamics Ltd www.oxfordbiodynamics.com	Diagnostics
ClinOx Ltd www.clinoxltd.com	Clinical trials
Eykona Ltd www.o3dt.com	3D imaging

Table 4: Oxford spin-outs post-1998

To this list must be added many companies set up by Oxford academics and researchers independently of the university.

Clearly the increased funding from the university has played an important role, but most of the credit must go to Tim himself. He understood how universities work and by force of his own personality and persuasiveness convinced the institution to embrace technology transfer at all levels. To do this he had to be accepted both in academic culture and the industrial sphere.

Technology Transfer In Oxford

Currently Oxford has over 100 people involved in research services and technology transfer. Inside the university the RSO has 36 staff, mostly graduates, with a third of these holding post-graduate qualifications. Within Isis, which is a limited company with the university as its sole shareholder, there is a staff of nearly 40, half of whom have doctorates and commercial or industrial experience, and a dozen of whom have MBAs. Some idea of the scale of the operation is indicated in Table 5.

Year Ending March -	2000	2001	2002	2003	2004	2005	2006	2007
University Investment	£1m	£1m	£1m	£1m	£1m	£1.2m	£1.2m	£1.2m
Staff	17	21	23	34	36	36	36	37
Open Projects	319	415	476	629	725	764	784	841
Patents filed	55	63	82	65	52	55	57	49
Licence Deals	21	36	42	37	31	38	45	50
Consultancy	–	–	–	34	50	48	59	89
Spin-outs	6	8	8	7	3	4	6	7

Table 5: Isis Innovation 2000-2007

The philosophy of Isis, developed by Tim, is to concentrate on those researchers who want to transfer technology. These researchers are encouraged by advertising and presentations, but potential spin-outs do not arise from having periodic technology audits. It is our view that these are counter-productive because one finds out what seems hot at a given instant and at other times the researcher loses interest. The model is to create on-going interest so that the subset of academics who generate new ideas and also have the drive to put in the work required for exploitation will approach Isis rather than the other way round. Of course nothing works better than a few successes and perhaps for this reason the Chemistry Department produces a lot of companies. The younger researchers can see that some of their older colleagues have become wealthy, but without giving up their university posts or the academic imperatives. Most often it is the post-doctoral researchers who have joined the fledgling companies, again often very advantageously.

The Leeds Model

It would be wrong, however, to think that the Isis model is the only one, or that it is obviously the best mechanism for technology transfer in all cases. The University of Leeds, which is one of the most successful UK institutions in this respect, has adopted another route. Whilst retaining within the university the identification and protection of the intellectual property, they outsourced the technology transfer function to external company Techtran. Techtran covers the entire transfer encompassing licensing, creating spin-outs and the building of the newly created companies, including sourcing finance. The case for this alternative approach, which is particularly strong for smaller institutions, is not just that it may save money, but more importantly the university is supported by a group with significantly increased competency – a team including experts with financial and management consultancy backgrounds. They are likely to have sufficient experience to be able to make good judgements in licensing or spin-out options. Techtran does for Leeds what Isis does for Oxford. Table 6 lists the Leeds spin-out companies created by Techtran.

Company	Main Business
Avacta Plc www.avacta.com	Detection and analysis of molecules
Luto	Patient information on pharmaceuticals
Green Chemicals Plc	Software for industry
Tracsis Plc www.tracsis.com	Resource scheduling for transport
DyeCat www.dyecat.com	Speciality polymer chemicals
Ovatus	Drug discovery
Chamelic www.chamelic.co.uk	Stimulus responsive polymers
Leeds Lithium Power www.leedslithiumpower.com	Polymer gel electrolytes
Leeds Reproductive Biosciences	Diagnostics for fertilisation
Dispersia www.dispersia.co.uk	Thermal transfer fluids
Tissue Regenix www.tissueregenix.com	Donor tissue

Company	Main Business
Icona Solutions www.iconasolutions.com	Software for industry
Getech Group Plc www.getech.com	Oil exploration services
Photopharmica www.photopharmica.com	Light sensitive drugs
Syntopix Group Plc www.syntopix.com	Topical antimicrobials

Table 6: Leeds University spin-outs created by Techtran

Whereas Oxford with Isis has more than 50 people in its technology transfer office, Leeds has none. Most UK universities tend to have between 5 and 20 employees. In the USA a group of between 10 and 30 make up the technology transfer office, with MIT, for example, having 29 people.

These bare bones give some indication of the frameworks within which spin-outs are created.

In the next chapter we examine the mechanics of setting up a company.

4

Starting A Spin-Out Company

It is probably best if the academic initiates the creation of a new spin-out company rather than some other person or body having to persuade him or her to do so. This is because it can be a very time-consuming and stressful business, as well as possibly distracting from normal research. The academic must want to do it.

In general the university may not grant permission for the academic to become an executive director – becoming a non-executive director or consultant is more common, although in some instances upon flotation some listing authorities have insisted on the academic becoming an executive research director. It is also the case that some funding bodies do not permit their funded researchers to take directorships.

It is also usually best if the academic does not join the company, but rather sticks to his or her day job in the university and is involved in the commercial venture as a non-executive director or as a member, perhaps chairman, of the Scientific Advisory Committee. Frequently, however, post-doctoral researchers from the research group that originated the technology do join the start-up company in technical roles.

Business skills are clearly vital and finding these, probably in the shape of a founding chief executive, is very important early in the process. Such a person will need time as well as skills and resources, and will need to sort out such things as premises, insurance and VAT registration, often with the help of local professional firms. The latter are increasingly to be found in the areas close to major research intensive universities. It is also true that the high legal costs and bureaucratic complexity of company formation in the UK represent a serious impediment to progress in this country.

Director's Responsibilities

A director's responsibilities are important and must be stressed. Directors protect creditors from the owners. They must not trade when the company is insolvent and must keep accounts that accurately reflect the financial position of the company. As directors they are trustees who must not benefit personally at the company's expense.

The simple checklist of what has to be done first is:

• decide what the company is going to do: what it will sell, to whom and how;

• decide upon who is going to own it;

• decide who is going to work in it;

• decide what funding is needed.

To assist in this process, the following initial questionnaire may be helpful.

The proposed business

Product/service offering

What product/services will the company sell in the short, medium and long-term?

Source of products/services

Where will the company get the products/services it sells (develop them, manufacture in-house, buy in, already has them, etc)?

Target market

Estimate the market's size: is it growing, static or declining? Identify potential competitors.

Route to market

How will the goods/services be sold?

Business projection

What are the expected sales, margins, overheads and cash requirement for the first few years? Banks may furnish *pro forma* spreadsheets and examples.

Company personnel

Give the names of individuals if known and state whether full or part time (quantify part time). State specifically who will be responsible for the following key functions:

- product development (R&D)/procurement;
- sales and marketing;
- finance/accounting;
- leadership/general management.
- Who are the proposed directors and company secretary?
- Who are the proposed lawyers, accountants and bankers?

Investment

- What is the total cash investment by external investors?
- Who are the external investors?
- What equity is offered to the university and the investors?

Risks

What are the major sources of risk/uncertainty in this proposal? (Technical risks, academic competition, commercial competition, management risks.)

The science and intellectual property

The purpose of these sections is to enable the university to understand and evaluate both the quality and the security of the science, in order to form an opinion of its potential value.

Add a section, which will describe, to a suitably qualified person, the basis of the science, the relevant experience of the scientists involved, and likely developments in the field.

Also describe both the intellectual property, and the know-how, which will be going into the company (including patents, both filed and potential). Identify any university intellectual property that will be needed by the company.

Ongoing research

Will the company place research contracts with the university? If so, enclose details of the duration and magnitude of the proposed projects. Have terms been agreed with the university?

The next stage is to develop a business plan, a process that will involve the academic inventor, the investors and ideally the proposed chief executive.

The business plan should include at least the following aspects:

- company management and structure

- staffing structure

- market

- manufacturing or production methodology

- product details and intellectual property

- financial forecasts

- competition

- risk and reward for benefactors

- how the product will be sold

- time scale and benchmarks

Particularly important is a clear, concise executive summary that emphasises the unique aspects of the company in a way in which a non-specialist investor can understand what is in it for him or her.

The Division Of Equity

At the earliest time possible it is also necessary to decide upon the equity split – how much of the shareholding will go to the investors, the academic and the university. Three-way negotiations are potentially difficult and it may be wise for each party to have its own legal advice, particularly as the final shareholders' agreement will be a significant legal document.

Most of what appears above is relatively straightforward, but involves a significant amount of work and time with the burden falling on the academic and the putative chief executive officer (CEO). Even more demanding and much less routine is raising the necessary funding.

Raising The Funding

Typical university spin-out companies start small and need funds in the range £500,000 to £2 million ($1-4 million). The ease of raising such amounts tends to be cyclical: relatively easy in some periods but desperately difficult in others. At any time this is rather an awkward level of funding. The old joke states that the sources of sums of this size are the three "Fs": family, friends and fools. There are still instances where the academic entrepreneur mortgages his or her house, but that is not common. Most university spin-outs are funded initially by "angels", who are often rich individuals that have made fortunes from high technology ventures. These wonderful people are often in contact with university technology transfer companies on the lookout for opportunities.

There are also venture capital firms whose business it is to invest their shareholders' money for equity – shares – in companies. Before making an offer venture capitalists will undertake very detailed due diligence, that is looking into all aspects of the proposal. In particular they will need to be certain about patents, details of the financial plan and evidence of market interest. They will certainly also come back with a number of enquiries. Since the amount of work they need to do is almost the same for a small company as for a larger one, venture capitalists are not usually interested in small start-ups. Where they do play an important and active role is in subsequent rounds of funding, when the start-up can demonstrate that it is a real, viable and potentially very profitable business.

The academic entrepreneur should not be too naive. The venture capitalist's duty is primarily to shareholders and so he or she will drive for the best bargain possible. A very silly but frequent error is to underestimate how much capital is required and then have to go back for more. If things are progressing well then the backer may produce more cash, but also increase their percentage of the ownership so that the founders get diluted. If this happens several times the founders may be left with a small, and rapidly vanishing, part of the ownership. Venture capitalists frequently also set milestones, so that cash is only provided when certain agreed results, perhaps sales, have been achieved.

From whoever the funding for the spin-out comes, a very important aspect will be the presentation of the case for funding. This will be by the scientific founder and the CEO: the former explaining in simple terms the technology, and the latter the business aspects. It cannot be stressed too strongly that backers of companies judge the people as the most important factor. Being able to give a presentation that displays enthusiasm as well as realism is vital.

Documentation

Once there is an agreed source of funds the actual setting up of the company has to become formal, and professional legal advice is essential. This involves a significant amount of documentation. Firstly a Heads of Agreement needs to be produced. This lays out the key provision of all aspects of the spin-out company and provides the summary from which the lawyers can build the full documentation.

The full documentation will start with the shareholders' agreement. This covers the relative shareholdings between the founding researchers; the university; management; and the investors. It will include any protections which each shareholder may insist upon.

With spin-outs from universities there is almost always a Technology Licence Agreement which authorises the company to use specified intellectual property owned by the university. Normally this agreement will state that the intellectual property returns to the university if the company were to be wound up.

The relationship between the academic founders of the company and the company itself is covered by a consultancy agreement which the university needs to approve. Given the fact that academic salaries are not very large, most universities are not concerned about their employees earning significant sums outside their normal academic duties of teaching and research. Indeed this is the only way to retain some research superstars. Where universities do take issue is in relation to the amount of time an academic may spend outside his or her normal duties. The University of Oxford, for example, has a normal limit of 30 days per year.

Other important legal documents essential in the setting up of a company include the managing director's Service Contract, which is supplied by the company's lawyers and agreed by the independent lawyer of the CEO, unless he or she has the confidence to act for him or herself. The Memorandum and Articles of Association are standard documents which set out the nature of the company's business and its operations. They include the rules of the company with the number and types of share the company can issue, the rights of shareholders and the powers of directors. There may also be documentation about any Share Option Schemes. Share options are rewards to the early management of the company which can be viewed as being merited because of the risks involved in working for a start-up company. They are also a form of gentle handcuff to dissuade the employee from leaving prematurely, when the options would be lost. This type of scheme may be set up after the company has got off the ground, but often it is done at the spin-out stage with, in particular, the vesting period, how long the shares must be held, and the option exercise price being defined.

Completion

Once all these documents have been prepared there has to be a final approval of completion, when each person involved has to sign all the paperwork. This is often the occasion for a few drinks before the real work starts. In the early days a lot of external advice may be needed over and above the company's lawyers. Principally this will come from banks, accountants and possibly public relations firms or business support networks. A key role of the CEO is to minimise expense. It will also be necessary to take out insurance including: directors' and officers' liability insurance; building and contents insurance; employer's liability insurance; public liability and product liability insurance. The company's accountants and bankers will give advice on the many taxation aspects of the new company. For the company these include value added tax; corporation tax; national insurance; and research and development tax credits.

The individuals involved in the spin-out should also consider and seek advice on their own personal tax situation and possible options that might reduce their liabilities. The key areas of taxation, all of which merit specialist advice, are: capital gains tax; income tax; the Enterprise Investment Scheme in the UK; and Enterprise Management Incentives. Finally, even at the early stage, it can be sensible to consider inheritance tax options.

As well as the managing director and chief executive officer, the company must also have a company secretary who reports to the directors, and is responsible, along with the directors, for keeping records of the company. Records will include notices of meetings and the minutes thereof, and returns which have to be made to the legal authority Companies House. The latter have an excellent web site: www.companies-house.gov.uk. Quite often the company's lawyers or accountants may be the company's secretary. It is very important to keep good records in a formal way since these may be vital at a later stage when the company is involved in a takeover or seeks major investment.

When the company gets started, rather like a baby, it changes very quickly in the early months of its life, and it is important to adapt as things change. This includes making management changes as the infant grows. Experience has shown that it requires very different entrepreneurial skills to get a start-up in motion from those required to run a business with a large number of employees. All these aspects will be illustrated in the next two chapters which are a real-life case study: Oxford Molecular, first a start-up spin-out and later a public company.

5

Oxford Molecular Ltd

Scientific Origins

My birth date was especially lucky. Being born on the first day of the last quarter of 1939, 1 October, meant that I missed national service by a day: a matter for regret at the time. It gave me an extra full year of salaried life as an Oxford academic since one retires on 30 September following one's 67th birthday. Above all, it meant that I completed my Oxford doctorate in 1964, at a time when academic jobs were very easy to get. Universities were expanding or being created all over the world and the flow of new positions seemed endless. It was a situation that lasted about three years. My doctorate was in physical chemistry, largely as a spectroscopist, but again due to the fortunate age, I was one of the first generation of graduate students to use a computer. The device was a Ferranti Mercury, a valve machine that filled a room despite only having a 32k memory and having to be addressed in the language of autocode. This machine, so primitive by contemporary standards, nonetheless enabled Dorothy Hodgkin to solve important crystal structures such as vitamin B12.

After the doctorate I became a Junior Fellow at Balliol and then spent a year in Paris doing some theoretical chemistry, again largely computational, calculating the properties of molecules containing only two atoms, such as nitrogen.

I returned to Oxford to a newly created Fellowship at my own college, Brasenose, where I have been ever since, teaching undergraduate chemistry and doing research in the Physical Chemistry Laboratory, I later became head of the Chemistry Department at Oxford, which is the biggest in the Western world.

At first I did some experimental research using lasers as well as theoretical work. However, I soon decided that Oxford was not a good place to do the experimental work as I was constantly beaten in the publication race by bigger, better-funded US laboratories. On the side of theoretical calculations, on the other hand, we were at no real disadvantage, and the supply of very high quality research students meant that it was possible to play in the world "first division". My work was rather pure, even perhaps a trifle esoteric – capable of impressing my colleagues and rivals in the game, but not really having much impact on the wider world.

I have always subscribed to the cock-up theory of history rather than conspiracy, and indeed moving as I did into the application of theoretical chemistry and computing to problems in biology and, above all, pharmaceuticals, was not a cleverly planned career move.

In the late 1960s I received a letter from Anthony Roe who was at the time working with Jim Black for the UK subsidiary of the US pharmaceutical company, Smith Kline and French. They were searching for compounds to block the action of histamine that causes secretion of acid in the gut: the so-called H2 activity, to distinguish it from H1 activity whereby histamine causes the symptoms of allergy, as in hay fever. Blocking acid secretion would, and famously, eventually did, cure stomach ulcers. This line of approach had been successful in Jim Black's hands when, with ICI, he had discovered the beta blockers which inhibit the action of noradrenaline on the heart. This work was later to gain for Jim (now Sir James Black) a well-deserved Nobel Prize. Like much of pharmaceutical research it is based on the simple but realistic view that drugs are almost invariably small molecules which work by binding to a big molecule, most often a protein. The drug binds tightly, the tighter the better, to a specific so-called binding site on the protein. The binding site has a distinctive shape, which is why some molecules bind better than others, and organic chemists have to synthesise large numbers of variants of the small drug compounds so as to optimise the fit between the partners.

Anthony had written to me to ask for my opinion on a theoretical paper which showed, using crude calculations, that the small histamine molecule can exist in two alternative shapes, and went on to propose that one shape of the molecule caused H1 effects and another the more interesting H2 reactions, there being two quite distinct histamine receptor proteins.

It was an area of which I knew next to nothing, but I could see that the calculations were almost trivial. One could see that two shapes were possible without using a computer, and that there were also two ionic forms and two other alternative structures known as tautomers. It could be that each shape hit one of the two receptors but there was no logical link.

To SKF this question was important enough for me to visit them in Welwyn and to become a consultant on the very outer fringes of their important work leading to the drug cimetidine, sold as Tagamet. From Jim, and in particular his chemist colleague Robin Ganellin, I gradually learned quite a lot about molecular pharmacology.

As a result of having my eyes opened to the fascinating world of small molecules in biology, I started to set research problems in this area for some of my own research students. Initially this was often for weaker students, or more particularly those who were more interested in the computing aspects than in the actual chemical problems.

By the mid-1970s at least half my group were working in this area, even though it was largely despised by purer theoretical chemists. A sabbatical year at Stanford enabled me to write a book entitled *Quantum Pharmacology* which was well received in some quarters, and marked my move more firmly towards the application of quantum mechanics, and later statistical mechanics, to drugs and to problems in molecular biology. Thereafter progress was hitched to advances in computer power.

When the first edition of *Quantum Pharmacology* appeared, our calculations were limited to considering individual small isolated molecules with no solvent or other surrounding molecules. They might have been isolated in interstellar space, but some interesting differences between molecules did emerge. More computer power permitted bigger molecules to be considered, until in the 1980s whole proteins and lengths of DNA could be simulated in computer calculations which now included an environment of water molecules and the ions which can be found in real-life situations.

By the late 1970s some of the more research-oriented companies were taking notice of this work, but did not employ their own specialists. In part this was because computing was done on big mainframe computers, available essentially free to the academic community but not cost effective for research in the pharmaceutical industry. A discontinuity in history came with the workstation, the single-user machine needing no operator or expensive air conditioning.

With some of the earliest workstations, which had black and white screens, my group succeeded in producing some colour graphics pictures of molecular structures. This was done by Valerie Sackwild, now an IBM vice president, who charmed technical help out of Lance Mangold, the photographer in Oxford's prestigious Biophysics Laboratory. The colour pictures were created by putting part of the picture on the screen, photographing through a red filter, winding back the film, then pulling up the rest of the image and photographing through a blue filter.

These colour graphic slides were rapturously received at conferences and helped open up the eyes of pharmaceutical companies to the possibilities in terms of helping the creativity of their chemists. The companies began to ask for copies of our software, which was passed on either for free or for a very small payment. This was not because we were dim, but because the software was not of commercial standard, not documented and certainly not supported. Some companies were, however, created in the early 1980s to satisfy this demand.

True colour graphics machines, first vector machines from companies such as Evans and Sutherland, and later raster machines pre-eminently from Silicon Graphics and later Hewlett-Packard, accelerated the growth of computer modelling and the application of theoretical chemistry as an aspect of drug research.

Interest From The Pharmaceutical Industry

By the end of the 1980s the subject was well established. All the world's major pharmaceutical, agrochemical and biotech companies were investing in workstations and software. In the first instance, this was to display and manipulate representations of molecules. At this level it is merely a high technological way of replacing the models with balls for atoms and sticks for bonds that chemists and students have always used. Of course, a sticks and balls protein model may take weeks to build; it is subject to gravity; it breaks or droops and it is impossible to see what is going on inside. With a graphics display model on a computer, however, none of these drawbacks apply, and there are other benefits too: the geometrical distances are not regular as when using a box of models, but true to the known experimental distances found from crystallograph; the model can be viewed in three dimensions; and motion may even be included, as in a real molecule.

The technique can, in addition, offer far more than pictures. With the procedures of theoretical chemistry, calculations can be made of, for example, just how tightly a proposed drug may bind to its protein receptor. This will relate to the value of the compound as a drug in terms of dose. Other relevant properties may be computed, as for instance the solubility of the putative drug in fat, an indicator of how easily it may cross a cell membrane to get to its target, or its reactivity with other chemical species.

Ideally, drug design would start with a knowledge of the structure of the big molecule and the all-important binding site to which the drug must attach itself. If this is cannot be deduced by experiment it may be possible to predict that structure using computational methods. One key approach is to use homology. The structure of a protein whose amino acid sequence is known from the easily determined gene sequence is built by comparing that sequence with sequences of proteins of known three-dimensional structures in a database.

Even when there is nothing known about the receptor structure, all is not lost. Enzymes catalyse reactions. If one wants to block a reaction then all that is needed is a molecule which will block the enzyme, which in turn acts by binding to and stabilising the highest energy structure along the path between reactant and product. Theoretical chemistry can lead to a prediction of that structure and software has been developed to design stable molecules which mimic the unstable structure stabilised by the enzyme. These stable mimics can act as drugs, a fact which nature uses with penicillin.

Traditionally the pharmaceutical industry found drugs by an intelligent use of "suck it and see". Often many thousands of molecules were synthesised by organic chemists and tested before a useful compound was discovered. In round terms this may cost £100 million, with a further £400 million to be spent before the compound reaches the public.

If computational techniques developed in universities can reduce these costs then surely there was the basis of a business, taking these ideas from academia and selling the software to the pharmaceutical industry or using it on their behalf to design new drugs. Having the basis of a business is, on the other hand, the easy bit. To create a company of any size requires someone special. It requires an entrepreneur. For Oxford Molecular that someone was Tony Marchington.

A Potential CEO

Tony Marchington sat the entrance exam for Oxford in 1971. He was interviewed at Brasenose by me and my legendary organic chemistry colleague, John Barltrop, who had also been my own tutor. Tony came from New Mills Grammar School in the Peak District, the oldest of three sons of a north Derbyshire hill farmer. We accepted him without hesitation, not so much because of outstanding academic achievement or even promise, but more because of his obvious character, toughness and flair.

His first term in Oxford started sensationally. During an organic chemistry practical class he had an accident and burned his hands quite seriously. They had to be bandaged so heavily that he had mitts like boxing gloves and was unable to hold a knife and fork, a problem that was surmounted by getting the college porters to feed him This meant that he did not have to miss any education and also he formed a strong bond with the porters, especially one John Watkins who later became head porter.

The undergraduate years were satisfactory from an academic point of view, and very successful from a social and sporting angle. Tony played football for the university, drank too much and created a lot of fun around him.

After final exams at the end of the third year, Oxford chemistry is unusual in that there then follows a year of research, the Part II, which contributes to the overall class of degree. Tony chose to do this year in my lab and was introduced to computational chemistry with a biological slant.

At that period I was a consultant to ICI Plant Protection, the agrochemical part of ICI, later part of Zeneca, and now Syngenta. Tony wanted to stay on to do a doctorate at the end of his Part II and we fixed up one of the first CASE awards for him, with Keith Heritage of ICI as his industrial supervisor. CASE, an acronym for Cooperative Award in Science and Engineering, is an excellent scheme whereby a research student works on a problem of interest to industry and spends part of his or her time at the industrial laboratory. When Tony took up one of the first of these scholarships they were often thought of as slightly second rate, but happily they are now much sought after as they have a financial supplement and often, as in Tony's case, lead to employment in the company. His project involved trying to design a fungicide that would work by blocking the enzyme cytochrome P450, a way of preventing fungus on cereals.

Research suited Tony, especially in my group and with my style of supervision, which he described as 'benign neglect'.

Giving him freedom to do other things enabled me to appreciate just what an entrepreneur he was. While a research student, he shared a flat with Walter Hooper, an American priest who had been C.S. Lewis' private secretary, and was the executor of the Lewis literary estate and even later advisor to the making of the film *Shadowlands*. In the late 1970s the American Baptists, who almost venerate Lewis, wanted to make a film about him. Walter Hooper produced a script but with some parts sublet to Tony. For this he earned £3,000, a lot of money for a graduate student at that time.

To my amazement he took his new wealth and went out and bought a steamroller. I thought he had gone quite crazy, until I learned that over the summer he was taking the steamroller to steam rallies and being paid handsomely for doing so. He had an eye for a bargain – he bought John Barltrop's Triumph Spitfire for £50, and ran it for several years, and used a college vacation grant to go to Bavaria and buy old BMW motor cycles, which are still stored on his father's farm.

The combination of successful science and business flair appealed to ICI who were very keen that he should join them and take our technology of primitive molecular design into the company. Despite the fact that this was during a recession when there was a no hiring policy and redundancies were the order of the day, ICI offered Tony the highest starting salary for someone at his stage of development that they had ever given.

Tony accepted and went on to set up what was the first industrial molecular modelling group in British industry: a rare instance where agrochemical research preceded pharmaceuticals in scientific innovation.

On the strength of his letter of appointment Tony went to his bank manager and borrowed £35,000 with which he purchased a pair of steam ploughs, massive steam engines which pull the plough between them on a chain, and are capable of ploughing what no tractor can manage. These too he took to steam rallies and earned even more.

Being an entrepreneur, however, he questioned himself as to how much the rally organisers made if they could pay him. So whilst still working with ICI he set up his own Buxworth Steam Group to run his own steam events. The first at Lymm in Cheshire made many thousands of pounds profit in a single weekend and caused a ten-mile tailback on the M6. This became a profitable side business while he was still an ICI employee. Gradually the steam business became more focussed on Edwardian fairground rides and associated engines. He bought and restored a steam carousel, found a rare centre engine for it and produced a ride for which Michael Jackson was later to offer $250,000. To this was later added a helter-skelter, the showman's steam engine The Iron Maiden, which featured in the film of that name, and a Wall of Death. His final steam engine triumph was to buy and restore the historic locomotive, the Flying Scotsman, former holder of the world speed record. This was made possible by the subsequent success of Oxford Molecular.

When the steam rallies were set up in a farmer's field, the beer tent was run by Tony's mother, but on a hot weekend with no mains power or water, keg beer kept chilled in a bath of iced water does not last well. This problem provides a vignette of Tony's entrepreneurial flair. He went, during the late 1980s recession, and bought a £40,000 refrigerated meat lorry from a receiver for £8,000. He took it to Morrells Brewery, who converted it at their expense into the perfect cellar, which he filled with their beer. After driving to the field, the refrigeration unit is switched on and within minutes the beer in the lorry is at the perfect temperature and goes to the pumps through insulated pipes. Being so well kept, it can be bought on a sale or return basis and the entrepreneur cannot lose.

Qualities such as these did not go unnoticed in ICI and within a couple of years Tony was moved from the research laboratories to the commercial side of the business and given training in management which was later to prove so valuable. His place in the research team was filled by another of my students, Sandra Robins.

Thinking About A Company

At about this time, in 1982, Tony came to see me with the idea of setting up a company to exploit our technology. The idea was simple. We would take the software developed in my group, tart it up as a commercial package, sell a few copies to pharmaceutical companies at a high price and retire rich. The idea was discussed seriously by him, myself and Sandra with our vague plan for me to provide software, Sandra to make it commercially acceptable and Tony to market, sell and run the business. One crucial meeting we held in the Oxford Club, Vincent's. At this meeting it was me that had cold feet. It seemed too big a risk for young people with good industrial jobs. We even had in mind a name, Molecular Design Ltd. Perhaps the final nail in that embryonic enterprise was the delivery to my desk in the laboratory of a flier announcing a new company in Hayward, California, Molecular Design Inc. Someone else had had a similar idea and even used the same name, so we dropped our plans. When four years later Molecular Design Inc was sold to Robert Maxwell for $49 million, I realised I had been wrong.

By the mid-1980s Tony's ICI career too was not as happy. Being promoted very rapidly causes jealousies and one can encounter company politics. Tony had been moved from product managing to selling in South America. This is an ideal stepping stone for a company man who is going places, but it was a strain and Tony is not the quintessential big company man.

When his patron did not achieve the top job and as a consequence all his protégés were blocked for a while, Tony was given the sound but fatal advice to keep his head down and his nose clean for a couple of years and then his time would come again. They could not have chosen a worse recipient for such a nostrum.

Since he had the steam engine business to fall back on, he was able to take the decision to resign. When doing this he came back to Oxford to talk it over with me, not I suspect for advice, but more to clarify his own thoughts by discussion. I agreed with him that it was not crazy to resign. I had never seen him staying in a multinational company as an employee for long. I did, however, offer the advice that steam engines would not prove to be mentally stimulating enough and what he really needed was a high tech business as well. Steam to provide cash and fun in the summer, but something more capable of creating wealth in the winter.

We did have a couple of ideas, most notably to try to exploit an ICI invention of Ron Coffee called electrodyne spraying, whereby agrochemicals can be administered as ions by squirting herbicides or other agrochemicals through a powerful electrostatic field that causes electrons to be stripped off. The ionised molecules then follow lines of force so that the back of a leaf gets covered as well as the front, and only very small amounts of chemical are used. Tony had the notion of using this idea to spray fungicide in motel rooms or even to administer deodorants, but the question of patents was not resolved and that idea fell flat.

Nonetheless he was now very receptive to ideas for a start up business and had time in the winter to do some preliminary work if the right proposition came along. In the winter of 1988 it did, largely as a result of the innovations due to Margaret Thatcher.

The Intellectual Property

Mrs Thatcher is now at the stage of her ex-premiership when it is fashionable to condemn all she did. People who complain about privatisation should remember that when she came to power the telephones were still part of the Post Office and one waited six months for a phone. She changed the climate for business and certainly was responsible for two innovations which were crucial to our starting a business.

The first important contribution she made was to change the tax regime so as to make it possible to have a venture capital source of funding in Britain. In a typically random way I became involved in this and learned about it very early in its history.

In the USA the chemical giant Monsanto had previously had a fairly successful venture capital fund to support fledgling high technology businesses, in part to keep a close watching brief on new technologies and also to make very respectable earnings. When the British climate changed in the early 1980s to encourage similar ventures here, Monsanto decided to set up a fund in London, using Deloitte as a consultant to help them. They gave an instruction to involve the better universities, on the grounds that the most successful American funds had been associated with institutions of higher learning.

Deloitte's consultant was the late John Winter and he contacted me to find out who in Oxford was the right person to talk to. As it so happened, at that time I chaired the University and Industry Committee, later to be abolished and swallowed by the university bureaucracy. That committee position enabled me to introduce Monsanto to the Brasenose bursar, Norman Leyland, and we organised a meeting of bursars, several of whom subscribed to the venture capital fund. The fund was half Monsanto money and the rest raised in England and managed by David Cooksey (now Sir David), the pioneer British venture capitalist who was the head of Advent and had wonderful contacts in the world of venture capital, not least with Peter Brooke in Boston. Monsanto also seconded one of their employees to work in Advent, an Australia-born American citizen Paul Bailey, later to prove crucial to our launch.

For my help in getting the Oxford contribution off the ground, David Cooksey made me a member of the Technical Advisory Committee for Advent, along with Sir Peter Hirsch, Sir Hans Kornberg and Professor Bruce Sayers. We were supposed to give technical advice and spot likely emerging areas. In this context I introduced Paul Bailey to my colleague Raymond Dwek, who was doing superb work in the area of sugar chemistry and biochemistry, named by him "glycobiology". It was deemed to be an exciting area but too early for setting up a company, although Monsanto did invest in the technology and later, with the help of Advent, set up Oxford Glycosciences. These glimpses of the realities of creating companies were very stimulating and made me receptive towards the idea of setting up businesses in the UK in the same way as I had seen during long spells at Stanford in the late 1970s and early 1980s.

Mrs Thatcher's second gift to enterprise came in 1987, I have no doubt encouraged by David Cooksey. This was to give the intellectual property rights on work done in universities, but funded by government research councils, to the university concerned, so long as they had a mechanism to exploit the work.

Oxford University, as we have seen, decided to set up its own organisation to exploit its intellectual property after a lengthy and somewhat futile set of committees. At last in 1987 Isis Innovation Ltd was set up: an independent company wholly owned by the university and initially funded with money from Advent, Legal and General, and another small fund. As previously mentioned, James Hiddleston was recruited from industry to be the managing director of Isis Innovation, and I was put on a short-lived management committee, later being made a director.

The first meetings of the committee were in the autumn of 1988 and we discussed just how the company should exploit the intellectual property.

Obviously licensing was likely to be one route, but we also talked of setting up companies in the way so successfully done in Silicon Valley and around Cambridge, Massachusetts. A question was just where to start. One possibility which occurred to me was to revisit the software idea. I realised that this would involve some work, but in November 1988 my wife died of cancer after an 18-month battle with the disease, and my own preferred therapy for trauma is to work. In my case at least, it is effective. The day after Jessamy's funeral I telephoned Tony about the company.

Setting Up The Company

In fact not much of the initial work fell on me, but I did arrange for Tony to come and talk to James Hiddleston. Tony stayed for a few days, sleeping in his aged Ford Zodiac. During the night some of Oxford's young yobs decided to break into the car and must have had the fright of their lives when they disturbed a not insubstantial Marchington with a pickaxe handle in his hand, a tangible link with the world of steam rallies.

James Hiddleston had looked at the computer software in my lab and had also seen work on antibody modelling in the group of Tony Rees researching next door in the Biophysics department. He saw that the two sets of software fitted together neatly and could form the basis of a business. In a very short time, largely spent in James' then home outside Oxford, Tony Marchington and James wrote a business plan for a company we tentatively named "Oxford Biosoft", although even at that stage we were not too happy with a name redolent of loo paper. "Oxford Molecular" was my invention, the name being suggested in my mind by the US company New England Nuclear. One unforeseen complication with the name was that when we were established Oxford

University Press tried to stop us using it. Despite the fact that the company was one-third owned by the university and had no publishing activities, they objected to our using the name of Oxford. For us the connection with the university was crucial so we did not give way. Neither did the Press who cost us tens of thousands of pounds in legal fees and were prepared to take us to the High Court.

The business plan benefited from the years we had apparently lost by not setting up the company in 1982. Then we would have taken one piece of academic software, turned it into a single all-singing, all-dancing major product to be sold at a high price. This route had been followed by these then existing companies in the field:

- Biosym of San Diego, which had grown from work by Hagler and others at UC San Diego.

- Tripos based in St Louis, which originated in the academic group of Garland Marshall and was linked with the hardware manufacturer Evans and Sutherland.

- Polygen in Cambridge, Massachusetts with software from the Karplus group at Harvard and Rod Hubbard's group at York University.

- The smaller Oxford company Chemical Design Ltd founded by Keith Davies.

We felt that instead of doing as these companies had done, taking a single piece of academic software and making a product, we would play that trick time and time again. Using our good academic contacts we felt it would be possible to find good novel software at the very forefront of the sharpest science, bring it up to commercial standards, market and sell, with royalties being paid to the academic authors – often impoverished graduate students. In this way we felt we would be able to create a stream of products from highly funded research departments but with little investment from us beyond perhaps funding some workstations and a few post-doctoral positions.

It did seem important to us to involve Oxford University in our plan, since not only would this avoid any complication about the ownership of the software developed in Oxford, but in addition it would add credibility to our efforts to persuade researchers in other universities to sign over their computer programs to us. In our initial portfolio there were four programs from my group: a modelling package to display molecules (NEMESIS), a distance geometry program to get three-dimensional structures from partial data (CONSTRICTOR), a molecular similarity program (ASP) and a very innovative protein structure prediction tool (CAMELEON). In addition, from the crystallography department we had the structure generation code (COBRA) and Tony Rees' antibody modelling program, which still needed more work before being close to being a marketable product.

The names of most of the programs had something to do with snakes. This may or may not have been a good idea. Certainly the names associated the programs with a single company, but they did not even hint at the nature of the product or the problem it was expected to solve. The origin of these names lay in the logo we adopted. To save money and time we took over one that I had designed as a cover for my book *Quantum Pharmacology*. It was intended to link quantum mechanics, represented by the Greek letter *psi*, and the snakes on the medical symbol, the caduceus.

As to premises, the university came up with a marvellous contribution, although one for which we did pay a commercial rent. This was a temporary terrapin building which had been the workshop for the Astrophysics Laboratory, newly moved as part of the reorganisation of physics. This hut we grandly named Terrapin House, largely as a joke, but since that term is not universally appreciated as a temporary building, we later had the fun of having important Japanese businessmen looking for what they expected to be something akin to Millbank, only to find a prefabricated hut. From my personal point of view and that of Tony Rees, the location was perfect, being within twenty-five yards of our laboratories. This enabled me to continue with my normal academic job but to step over to the company several times a day.

The business plan was beginning to take shape. We had a tentative name, a site, some potential products, and most importantly in Tony Marchington a potential managing director. We also had a candidate for the technical manager in David Ricketts, one of my former students who was the author of our modelling program. He had joined Glaxo after doing his doctorate with me, and then had joined British Biotechnology in Oxford to apply the very type of software that we were hoping to sell.

Finance

The only thing missing was the finance. Raising this was the task taken on by Tony. Armed with the business plan he approached Advent first. They and a number of other funds we approached turned us down. Our chief problem was that software was not an attractive venture since it is so dependent on people who may leave. Although in our case this should not have been very serious since our source of ideas was, and is intended to be, the worldwide academic community, this did make us think and, to an extent, recast our ideas. Even at that early time we envisaged a three stage company:

1. We would be a software house with our major customers being the pharmaceutical and biotechnology companies.

2. When we had a successful business, we would use our software and academic contacts to do research projects for major partners, coming up with drug candidates.

3. Finally, we would use our skills on our own behalf to produce patented drug products which we would licence on. This would of course involve us in ultimately setting up a synthetic or medicinal chemistry company with its own laboratories.

After several unsuccessful attempts to raise the £200,000 we felt we would need, we approached Paul Bailey who had moved from Advent to be a partner in the Barings venture capital arm, Baring Brothers Hambrecht and Quist. He was interested and came to Oxford to go through our plans and produce detailed financial forecasts. It was at one of these meetings that we did succeed in producing the name for the company that satisfied us all and hinted that our intentions went beyond being solely concerned with software or even just pharmaceuticals. Oxford Molecular Ltd had all we wanted.

James Hiddleston brought us another investor in the form of Roderick Hall who became our staunchest backer, and ultimately chairman, when flotation was on the cards. He had a successful record as an investor in US high technology companies, including Sun Microsystems, and brought ambition as well as experience. From the start, Rod wanted to create a major international company. Paul Bailey brought the US fund AMT of Delaware Peter Walmsley to the table, a British venture capitalist with a particular interest in materials and a background in Dupont.

The final plan on which the business was set up took in £350,000 of capital for a third of the business, with the founders having about one-third between them and an equal amount being given to the university. Since the ambition was to create a serious company, we appointed as lawyers Booth and Co of Leeds (now Addleshaw Goddard, part of Norton Rose), and accountants KPMG Peat Marwick, both of whom would be credible when we came to go to the City if we succeeded.

In Business

All legal formalities were completed in the summer of 1989 and we opened up in Terrapin House on 1 September. There were just three employees: Tony Marchington, David Ricketts and a secretary. There was enough money to last a matter of months, so it was clearly going to be a real test. This was the first of the modern Oxford spin-outs in which the university held equity.

Some of the precious £350,000 had to be spent immediately on such mundane items as desks, carpeting, security – including a safe – and minimal decoration of the premises. Even though Tony had managed to negotiate three years of free auditing, it was obvious from the start that cash would be tight. We did, however, have a formal opening of the premises by Sir Richard Southwood, vice-chancellor of Oxford University.

Considerable work had to be done on the academic programs before they were in a fit state to sell, and calculations showed that we would need to be selling products within six months of the launch. This demanded a serious effort from a team of programmers who we were in no position to hire. The solution was to use contract programmers. Among the authors of the first batch of products was my student Andrew Smellie, whose then wife Penny, an Oxford physics graduate, was at that time working for a software contract house called Tessela. Tessela were particularly strong in the area of computer graphics, having done a lot of work with the government laboratories at Harwell and the Joint European Taurus experiment at Culham.

From Tessela we contracted six programmers managed by David Marsh, yet another Oxford-trained chemist. They quickly moved into Terrapin House and within the year transferred amicably from Tessela to become employees of Oxford Molecular. Despite the pressure they did achieve the target of having software ready to sell within six months.

Some of the workstations were purchased at favourable rates from a sympathetic Silicon Graphics Inc, but we were helped even more by Hewlett-Packard who remained staunch supporters of the company throughout the early years, in particular in the person of Denis Berger of the HP European headquarters in Geneva.

Not long before our launch, Hewlett-Packard had taken over Appollo and thus had a big effort in producing workstations. Denis, a biological scientist who had been previously with Biogen, had responsibilities which included the pharmaceutical and biotechnology area. The computer-aided molecular design business was growing rapidly, but it was difficult for Hewlett-Packard to make much impact, despite the excellence of their hardware, since they did not have any software to demonstrate to the molecular modelling community. Tony's skills as a deal maker were quickly in evidence as he managed to negotiate with Hewlett-Packard the first of a number of porting deals. These consisted of transferring our software so as to work on the Hewlett-Packard workstations and to join with them in demonstrating the power and quality of their machines to individual customers and at trade shows, often associated with scientific congresses or meetings. This income was vital in the early days, but on its own would not have been sufficient to tide us over until our sales volume grew sufficiently to make us profitable, especially as investment in new software was both vital and expensive.

Special Deals

Tony's second major source of income was what we termed "special deals". The idea was to go to a small number of pharmaceutical and biotechnology companies, with whom we had close relations from earlier academic collaborations, and make an arrangement whereby, for a significant upfront sum, the company would receive all our future products free of charge, although not free of support and maintenance. Initially we had made such an arrangement with Glaxo and with British Biotechnology, and later added similar contracts from Roussel and SmithKline Beecham.

It was not just cash that came from these relationships. They were genuinely special. It was possible to let these customers have source code and to encourage them to feed back information about weaknesses in the products and make suggestions about improvements to the extent of guiding us as to what the product should be and what they ideally would like.

Academic customers pose a particular problem for companies in our area of computational chemistry and molecular modelling. The tactic of our more established and bigger rivals at the time of our going into business was to sell to academics at massively discounted prices, but not passing on the valuable source code, only the usable binary code. Unfortunately, the academic customers expect to receive the same service and twenty-four hour help as companies who are paying very large sums for the same software. Our approach was to use a government funded scheme called CHEST (Combined Higher Education Software Team) for UK universities. The CHEST scheme, run from the University of Bath, was provided with all our software for a single fee. Distribution of the software was in their hands, so servicing this important but non-profitable sector did not detract our own small team from more urgent tasks.

We took the essence of the CHEST scheme to provide our own in-house service for all other worldwide academic sites. We named our scheme ASSIST. For any single university, for an annual fee of as little as $3,000, we would provide our complete range of software and a set of manuals to one named individual. Within the university they were at liberty to copy as often as they wished, but only the one named person could deal with us. In this way we avoided every single graduate student ringing up every time he or she encountered a problem, but the university got a fantastically cheap source of state-of-the-art software.

This was not pure philanthropy since we did receive a steady, predictable income stream, but more importantly this helped our growing reputation of being friendly to universities – it encouraged academics to see us as the appropriate vehicle to exploit their own software, and it was considered as "bread on the water". The more graduate students who used our software, the more in due course they would want to use it when they became employed in industry at some future date. We regarded these long-term relationships as very important, and also found that our close association with the University of Oxford gave credibility and authority to our claim to be on the side of the academics.

Scientific Advisory Panel

A two-way flow of ideas and information was also the motivation for another of our innovations, the ISAP – International Scientific Advisory Panel. We collected a number of distinguished academics active in the field and the leaders of the molecular modelling groups in our special deal companies as a panel to guide our science. The group played a very important role in the early days of the company and was chaired for us by Andy Vinter, who had experience both at Wellcome and then SmithKline Beecham, but at about the time of our opening had gone freelance. More recently he was a founder of Cresset, the UK drug discovery company. A crucial and wonderful contributor was Frank Blaney, a near genius modeller from Beechams, later Smith Kline Beecham and subsequently GlaxoSmithKline. At Tony's suggestion Frank wrote a brilliant structure-activity program for us, which is still widely used. He did this in his own time on a Silicon Graphics workstation provided by us. It was delivered to his home just before Christmas by Tony dressed as Santa Claus, accompanied by Dave Ricketts dressed as an elf, much to the amusement of Frank's daughters. Over the years this panel grew until, by the time of our flotation in 1994, our membership included three Nobel prize-winners. The first of whom was the Master of Balliol College, Barry Blumberg and later Rich Roberts and Jim Watson. Once again this was not done for short-term benefit but for long-term excellence in respect of the science we would be delivering.

Japanese Partners

Our notion of planning for the long-term, even though money could not be splashed around, was also important when we came very early on to develop a presence in Japan. Our investor Peter Walmsley had contact with the Japanese firm Toray who are basically a textile company with historic connections with Courtaulds and ICI. Amongst their companies there is also a computer business, Toray Systems Ltd, and through Peter we made arrangements for them to act for us in Japan. Once again to help our cash flow the deal was set up in such a way as to get them to provide some cash upfront for programs they would sell in Japan as an advance on royalties.

Making the deal was tremendous fun. In particular Brasenose College made Tony Marchington a member of the Senior Common Room and this enabled us to entertain visitors from time to time. The Toray representation, headed by Mr Tajima, were intelligent and sophisticated, well used to dining in fine restaurants and good hotels, but they very much enjoyed hospitality in the Senior Common Room of an Oxford College with its aspects of folklore. Silver candelabras, fine wines and, above all, the snuff delighted and amused them. So successful were our negotiations following these occasions that we took to referring to the "magic snuff" as a key ingredient in our public relations policy.

Advisors

Public relations were, and are, obviously important, but a company being run on a shoestring needs to be careful. We used a small local firm to produce our publicity and sales material, and another small PR firm, Andrew Lloyd Associates of Brighton, to provide low budget PR support.

The board of the company was initially chaired by James Hiddleston but in 1990 I took over and remained as chairman until the flotation became a real possibility, at which time Rod Hall assumed the role. Tony had to be company secretary as well as managing director, finance director and sales director. We did have some part-time bookkeeping help from a retired college accounts clerk, but I think we gave Gerrard Hodge of KPMG Peat Marwick a hard time in the early years. Regulations seemed incredibly onerous for a tiny company with so much to do and so few people to do what was necessary. With hindsight, however, the disciplines imposed on us were all very valuable and we became more appreciative as time went on.

Our bankers, Barclays, too were very understanding and patient. Area manager, Peter Burridge, referred to Tony as a 'hairy-arsed northerner', but he could see the talent in him and gave us lots of support and the occasional overdraft. In fact, so good were our relations with the bank that they used a picture of Tony with his most magnificent steam engine, The Iron Maiden, as publicity material during the time when the banks were under criticism for not being helpful enough to small businesses. We could truthfully say that they were supportive.

Sales

The first product to be ready was a modelling system to work on the Apple Mac. The intention had been for this to be a sort of central hub, the interface from which our other programs might run. This core program we thought might be called Medusa since the other programs were named after snakes. This neat idea came to nothing when we found that we could not register Medusa as it already belonged to someone else. We had to spell CAMELEON without an "H" for similar reasons. The modelling program, originating in Dave Ricketts' DPhil work in my group, was in the end stuck with its in-house name NEMESIS, the origins of which no one can now recall.

The first attempt to develop a sales force in addition to Tony was to recruit yet another of my former students, Clare Macrae, who had joined the Cambridge Crystallographic Database run by Olga Kennard. How we imagined that a lone young woman could set up a sales system and generate sales to support what was soon to be a dozen people is difficult to discern. It was a very naive move on our part and not a kindness to Clare who soon decided to return to Cambridge.

Our next attempt was to hire a hardened veteran, David Chapman, who had worked for several companies in the area including Chemical Design and American competitors. He did have the self-confidence to get things moving, even though by sheer mischance we had set up a company just after the stock market crash and at the start of a long recession. Sales were slower than we had anticipated and converting some of the academic code into saleable product took longer than expected. We also learned one general truth about our fledgling industry: nothing gets sold over the summer holiday period, so paying the wage bill in September became an annual headache.

Despite this, the company advanced throughout its first eighteen months without the need for any extra funding. It grew until the spring of the following year, 1991, at which time Terrapin House was overcrowded and very uncomfortable, especially in hot weather with all the computers running.

We had reached a state where we could go to our venture capitalists with evidence that Tony could run a company with tight budgeting: no frills, no company cars, people working long hours, but a viable business. The time had come for expansion and this started with a move to new premises.

Expansion

The timing of our move was propitious, not just for us, but also for the newly founded Oxford Science Park. From 1978-1988 I had been chairman of the University and Industry Committee. In that role I had been approached by several developers hoping to set up Science Parks in Oxford following the successful model in Cambridge by Trinity College, amongst others. Most of the would-be developers really just wanted to use the name of the university to ease planning restrictions. Indeed, the planning authorities were the main stumbling block. The countryside surrounding Oxford is more sensitive than that around Cambridge, and at least half a dozen schemes had been rejected on planning grounds.

The exception was a new Science Park to be developed on land owned by Magdalen College which was in an area zoned for industrial development. The college, with the Prudential as partners, set about developing a perfect site, near the city ring road with some 150 acres of rather poor land available. They succeeded in attracting the Japanese electronics company, Sharp, to set up in their own exclusive building, but also speculatively built the Magdalen Centre, a home for small start-up high technology science-based companies. The centre provided flexible lettings and communal facilities such as meeting rooms, a cafeteria, a reception and security. It was ideal for our purposes, although by no means inexpensive. The move and an expansion of both our technical and sales staff would require more funds.

Our venture capitalists, led by Barings, were encouraging. At a meeting in July they agreed to provide the extra funds required at a share price that was very attractive to us, being double the price they had paid at our foundation less than two years previously. Most importantly we also persuaded the university to invest in this second round. The curator of the University Chest, effectively the university finance director, Ian Thomson, agreed to invest £250,000 and in this way essentially maintained the university's share of the equity of the company.

On the basis of these promises the move was made during an August weekend. All the staff worked on the Saturday and Sunday and got the whole job completed in time to have a barbecue on the Sunday evening. We opened for business on the Monday morning with no down time.

Having purpose-built offices was a shot in the arm, as was the security of the promised extra funds. Some of the new cash was earmarked for the hiring of a professional full-time finance officer, who was found with the aid of headhunters. Our backers preferred us to go for a young, recently qualified chartered accountant, rather than an older, more experienced man. With hindsight they were probably wrong.

We too made some misjudgements. A further intention for the new funding was to open up offices in the USA. Our plan was to send Dave Ricketts to set up a sales office in Delaware where he could get help from Peter Walmsley. At the last minute we got cold feet, thinking that the task we were presenting was too difficult. This was a severe disappointment to Dave who soon afterwards resigned and joined our largest rival, Biosym Corporation of San Diego, only to rejoin us nearly three years later.

A major source of our caution was the realisation that money was still very tight and we were in our usual period of very few sales during July and August. This point was not lost on our venture capitalists.

Dealing with the venture capitalists

The night before our September board meeting Paul Bailey rang to say that, on going through the figures and bearing in mind that we were slipping behind budget, they would provide the promised extra finance but at a price of £1.14 per share not £2.28. This was something of a bombshell and made us feel that we were being screwed since the expenditure was already committed. We had to have the money, but we were prepared to fight. Having had a vague suspicion that something of this nature might occur, we had spoken to other potential backers. Nothing had been promised but it did give us enough confidence to have a short blazing row in which we offered to buy out our venture capitalists. The bluff worked. They paid the higher price and all was sweetness and light from then on.

Nonetheless it had been a salutary lesson for us and we determined to strengthen the board with someone who understood the game but was not one of our financial supporters. We mulled over a range of possible non-executive directors and finally decided upon Keith McCullagh, the managing director of nearby British Biotechnology Ltd, one of our special relationship companies.

Keith and his chairman, Brian Richards, had been senior executives at the UK subsidiary of the American pharmaceutical company G.D. Searle, based in High Wycombe. When Monsanto bought Searle for $2.7 billion it closed the UK company making everyone redundant. Most of the employees had been snapped up by UK pharmaceutical companies, but Brian and Keith, along with a handful of colleagues, raised the finance to found British Biotechnology in Oxford, later changed to British Biotech, a company which has had a very chequered subsequent record.

At the time we admired much of what they had achieved and saw them as being some way down a road that we hoped to follow. Advice from such a source would be invaluable, so we approached Keith. To our pleasure he accepted, but not before doing a detailed due diligence of Oxford Molecular and going through our books and board minutes. When he accepted, he warned us that he would not make life easy for us and would demand stringent financial controls and budgeting. He was as good as his word and did indeed insist on matching detailed budgets. Quite early on after a session with him in his own boardroom, Tony had to come back to our company and make five people redundant. It was tough, but in the end it was what the company needed. At the same time, it was a little difficult to take when our losses were quite small, while those of British Biotechnology ran into millions.

Overseas Sales

One way in which it proved hardest to meet budget predictions was with sales in the USA. As with many other European high-tech, companies, penetrating the world's largest market proved to be very difficult. Our first major effort in this respect was to hire Stefan Unger who had been with Silicon Graphics Inc, increasingly the dominant force with hardware in the molecular modelling world. Stefan had done research in the area himself, and during his time with Silicon Graphics had charge of marketing to the pharmaceutical and biotechnology industries. He opened up offices in Palo Alto, which seemed the ideal location, and had a spectacularly successful first few months. Sadly this was not sustained and we realised that that success had been based on cherry picking – going first to those potential customers with whom he already had close relationships. Stefan is above all a marketing man rather than a salesman, and in that respect did very well, but our needs were for sales to increase revenue.

In Europe those sales did come and always on forecast. This was a direct result of hiring Paul Davie, yet another Oxford Chemistry PhD, who had researched in Germany before joining Chemical Design, from whom he joined Oxford Molecular. Soon David Chapman moved on to run his own company and Paul took charge of sales. Due to his efforts we did get the company into profit for the first quarter of 1993.

Product Management

Another crucial appointment came gradually. One of the first extensions of the university base beyond Oxford and Bath, to which Tony Rees had moved as Professor of Biochemistry, was to Nottingham. There our chief contact was David Jackson of the pharmaceutical department, himself a modeller with expertise in forcefields and, more importantly, in pharmaceutical chemistry. David was interested in running courses for the company using multimedia techniques to train up chemists in industry. Soon David was spending more and more time with the company and grew into the role of product manager. After a while this became official and the company financed a replacement for him in Nottingham to fulfil his teaching requirements, although he continued to direct a research group.

Amongst the important new products attracted, as the net was cast wider, was the relational database of protein structures largely created in the research group of Janet Thornton at Birkbeck College, and later University College London. Janet is now head of the European Bioinformatics Institute in Cambridge. This was commercialised with the agreement and cooperation of British Technology Group, who had rights to the product (which is named IDITIS). It became one of the most successful products and one of Janet's former students joined the company, largely to oversee its development and updating. Less successful was another protein database originating in Leeds University, with whom our interaction was less fruitful.

The Materials Area

One question during the expansion period between 1991 and 1993, to which we constantly returned, was what to do about the area of materials. We had originally named the company Oxford Molecular not just to include using software in the pharmaceutical area as well as selling it, but also so as to include the very important topic of new materials. Indeed it was only because of this interest that Peter Walmsley had originally invested. Our expert in this subject was Elizabeth Colbourn.

Elizabeth had been the very last graduate student of the famous theoretical chemist, Charles Coulson. Indeed, he died before she had completed her thesis and I inherited her as a student for her final few months. After gaining her doctorate, Elizabeth did post-doctoral research in Canada and at Southampton, before joining ICI first at Runcorn and later at Wilton where she headed a modelling group. That strong group was researching advanced materials, many of which found their way into sophisticated military hardware such as stealth bombers. The peace dividend after the fall of the USSR produced a marked downturn in that business, leaving many of the ICI researchers unsettled and able to opt for generous redundancy or transfer terms.

Thus it was that Elizabeth joined us to head up our materials division, albeit a division of one, but with ambitious plans. She spent considerable time making academic contacts so as to repeat the successful strategy we had adopted in the biological scene, and produced a detailed and convincing business plan. The problem was that, with a total staff of under thirty, there was just not enough critical mass to make a real go of another area. It was too much to ask of a very small sales force to expect them to learn up another scientific discipline.

After months of vacillating, we decided that our real future did lie in the pharmaceutical and biotechnology field, and so Elizabeth set up an independent company, Oxford Materials, but one with close and friendly links and some small overlap in products.

The French Connection

If America was consistently difficult in the early days, our experiences in France were quite the opposite. One French rival whom we encountered at trade shows was Roger Lahana who had, while working for Pierre Fabre, developed an excellent modelling package christened MAD and a structure-activity program named TSAR. These packages were particularly popular with French industry, but Roger was essentially a one-man band, and with a limited product line. He was persuaded to join Oxford Molecular with his software and opened up a French office for us. This office became the first company to occupy the science park associated with the École Polytechnique in Palaiseau on the south side of Paris.

As well as Roger we had another French competitor, the Strasbourg based company Biostructure. This company had many parallels with ourselves, being associated with university professors in Strasbourg, Pierre Oudet and Dino Moras – both very well respected and producing some excellent software with, in particular, good graphical interfaces. They too sold very little in the USA and were not doing very well in Europe, despite having the support of some of the major academic figures in Europe, including Wilfred van Gunsteren of Groningen, and later Zurich, and the Nobel laureate Jean-Marie Lehn.

Having just become profitable early in 1993, it was possible to persuade our venture capital backers, and especially Rod Hall, that a takeover or at least a merger with Biostructure was a sensible option. Rod was beginning to show real faith in the company and had ambitious plans.

Tony succeeded brilliantly in doing a deal with the French judge who was handling the administration of Biostructure, which was in financial difficulties. The company was funded from the private funds of the Rémy Cointreau family and the venture capitalists Sofinova and Eurocontinental. Tony persuaded all three to contribute funds to support the enlarged company. All three parties attended our board meetings as observers and contributed enormously to the development of our business. At the same time the acquisition provided new intellectual property, new customers and a presence in the important German market through Biostructure's established sales office, while also expanding the vital academic network.

Business was starting to thrive. One major contribution was the brainchild of David Jackson. This was a scheme called MERIT, which provided a new method of licensing software. For an annually renewable subscription, a non-exclusive licence is granted, allowing the customer to use a given selection of the company's software at a single site. Even products under development could be made available under the scheme, and the feedback incorporated or the lack of interest noted and acted upon. The fee, being within customers' maintenance budgets, was more easily renewed than would be the purchase of new software in hard times.

Contract Research

By the summer of 1993 things were looking good. Biostructure had been absorbed and the consequent rationalisations made. Sales were growing. The time was approaching to start on what had always been the plan for the second leg – the contract research business. This was achieved with the antibody modelling software originating in Tony Rees' group. Despite being one of our most innovative and exciting products, the sales had been disappointing. It was clear that there were potential customers, but it seemed they would prefer to have us use the programs on their behalf, rather than buy in hardware, software and specialist personnel. Tony Rees and his group successfully humanised an antibody in a contract with the west coast biotechnology company Neorex.

For some time Tony Marchington had been getting consultancy advice from Jeremy Brassington, whom we had first met when the latter was a colleague of Paul Bailey at Barings. Now he was working largely on his own behalf and advising us. He came up with the notion that the time was ripe to float the company, turning Oxford Molecular Ltd into Oxford Molecular Group Plc.

6

Oxford Molecular Group Plc

The IPO

The summer of 1993 was seen by many as a window of opportunity for the flotation of companies, an initial public offering (IPO) on the London Stock Exchange. A number of smart people got companies listed on the London Stock Exchange, raising large sums of money. For research-based and loss-making high technology companies, the period was even more propitious. The relaxing of listing requirements, to a large extent pioneered by British Biotechnology, prompted several entrepreneurs to follow their example and seek a listing. It seemed that this could not go on indefinitely and this expansive period was likely to be followed by a time when the door would be firmly shut: a feeling enhanced by what seemed to us to be the rather dubious quality of some of the businesses being floated. Clearly the City was not very wise when it came to technological questions.

Although we did talk with some of the famous City institutions, our appetite for going public was definitively whetted by a presentation from Henry Cooke Corporate Finance of Manchester in the person of Martin Robinson. They were introduced to us by Jeremy Brassington, but were already familiar to some of us as one of the biggest provincial stockbrokers. In fact Brasenose College had a connection with them through the Hulme Trust, managed by Henry Cooke, and of which the college and Oxford University are major beneficiaries. The fact that the firm was a northern outfit commended it to us, as did their clear realism.

Martin's presentation explained the process of seeking a listing and claimed that this could, in principle, be achieved in as little as eight weeks, a feat that had been accomplished with Tadpole Technology. He largely won over an initially sceptical board. The only real reservation came from Keith McCullagh and he chose this time to withdraw from being a non-executive director. His major reason was pressure for him to concentrate on the development of British Biotechnology, which was entering the serious and exciting phase of their business when clinical trials of new drugs were looming. These drugs could have made the company, but in the event proved more than disappointing.

The rest of the board and our observers from the venture capital funds who supported us were strongly in favour, even though, as Martin Robinson explained, all the shareholders would be subject to a lock-in of perhaps a couple of years so that we could convince the City of our serious long-term commitment to the company. A decision to go ahead in principle was taken in November 1993, with a definitive date set for the irrevocable decision to be taken early in 1994.

The decision provoked a number of consequences and a massive amount of work for a total staff of only thirty. Henry Cooke had to do considerable due diligence on the company and here our original decision to employ top-level accountants and solicitors paid off. All the board meeting minutes and papers, contracts with employees and customers, and financial records were in excellent order for a small start-up company.

Rod Hall became chairman and we were advised that the Stock Exchange would require us to have a managing director, in addition to Tony as chief executive officer, a finance director of suitable experience, and at least one more non-executive director with genuine credibility in the City. This last addition to our ranks was the easiest to make. After flirting with names like John Harvey-Jones we followed the advice of Rod Hall and approached Christopher Weston, the chairman and CEO of auctioneers Phillips, and Rod's co-director at Foreign and Colonial Enterprise Trust. Christopher, being a man of experience, also did his own due diligence on us so as to be sure that he was getting involved with a company that had a really big future.

Going public is an expensive business, particularly if the attempt were to fail, so it was necessary to take in more funds. This was done in three tranches as various milestones were passed, with about £1.5 million being taken in November 1993, January 1994 and March 1994. By this stage, of course, with a flotation in sight it was not difficult to raise funds, and at a price which put a substantial value on the company.

New Employees

Finding the managing director who would report to Tony, and an experienced finance director, was not as straightforward and necessitated the use of headhunters. The first position to be filled was that of the MD and chief operating officer. At the end of the search our advisers came up with yet another Brasenose chemist, Tim Cooke, who had spent most of his career after an Oxford doctorate with Logica, although he joined us from OASIS management consultancy. His contract permitted him to start in February 1994, only about three months before the float.

The timescale was even tighter for the new finance director, Andrew Maunder. He had held various accounting positions with Racal Electronics, the Bentall Group in Canada and Motorola prior to joining 3NET Ltd, a supplier of digital networks. He joined in March, a month before we had to approach the City institutions. Fortunately, we had also recruited a financial controller in 1993, Diana Audley, who had a degree in physics as well as having trained with Coopers and Lybrand. It was on her that much of the heavy work fell in the preparation of the long-form report and audit required by the Exchange.

Verification

The verification procedure demanded for every single statement in these documents makes it hard to understand how any swindle, such as that perpetrated by Robert Maxwell, can be possible. So many people have to be involved in the process and our lawyer, which in practice meant Neil Woolhouse of Booth and Co, insisted upon documentary evidence for every single statement. We were not permitted to say in the prospectus that we were the biggest provider of software for computer-aided molecular design in Europe, even though we were, because that is hard to prove with documentation. On the company side we employed Andrew Stamp of Morgan Hands Burroughs to assist in the preparation of all the documentation. The small team did a fantastic job and our timetable only slipped about three weeks. We had aimed for the end of March, but in the end put back the date until the end of April.

Some things which we had anticipated to be minor took up a lot of time. Amongst these was the cover of the prospectus. Although we were a software company which did sell computers as a small part of the business, we were not allowed by the Exchange rules to put a picture of a computer workstation on the document. We had to go for something a little more abstract that attempted to show our software was related to molecular biology and drug design. When that was finally done and we had our draft, or "red herring", prospectus ready and a date from the Exchange for the listing, we were ready to do the roadshow, visiting financial institutions to try to persuade them to invest.

The Roadshow

The first port of call was the offices of Henry Cooke in Manchester. This was not just a dress rehearsal, but also an opportunity to sell the idea to the fund managers of Henry Cooke who look after the investments of their private clients. The plan was for 25% of the offering to be available to these private clients and the rest to City institutions with the general public getting its chance only when dealing started.

The presentation, which we could give as a slide show, or from a prepared set of reproductions of the slides mounted in a turn-over folder, was timed to take 20 minutes. This timing was important since we often made the presentation perhaps four or five times a morning, with taxi dashes between venues. We were accompanied by Richard Lucas of Henry Cooke who acted as our minder, ensuring that we did not make statements about profits nor anything not included in the prospectus.

The actual presentation was in three parts. Tony Marchington spoke first, and tried to explain what the business was about. To do that he started by talking about Brunel and the bridge which had to be built over the Thames at Maidenhead by the Great Western Railway. At the last moment Brunel had been instructed that only one pillar was to be allowed. This required the longest, flattest brick arches ever built and the experts had thought that this was impossible, even turning up when the scaffolding was removed to see it collapse. However, because of its design and mathematical perfection it did not fall and still carries the railway today. From this he moved on to molecular design and gave an outline of our vision.

The central portion of the show was a brief description of our science, given by me. The final section, again delivered by Tony, came to the prospects, the market and our plans both for our MERIT scheme and the contract research business. In this last area we were able to quote the success of the contract to humanise antibodies and to make a convincing tale of the possibilities of doing research contracts for pharmaceutical companies.

The team that went on the roadshow trip was Tony, one of us two scientists and Andy Maunder. Despite his very brief time with the company he managed to pick up not only the finances but also a good notion of our activities. He also ran a book on our impressions of how the presentations had gone. After each we estimated just how much each fund manager would invest. That was very hard to judge. People who seemed fascinated did not necessarily come in, while others who seemed bored did so. A fair indication of just how difficult a judgement that was can be ascertained by the fact that I won the contest, despite being certainly the least qualified to guess.

The roadshow proper started in Scotland, Glasgow in the morning and Edinburgh in the afternoon. As well as the presentation team, we had two teams from the technical part of the company. Leapfrogging each other, one of these technical teams came to each presentation and were there set up complete with a workstation and demonstrations of the software prior to our arrival. When we dashed off to the next venue the technical people stayed on, gave demos and in a number of cases really helped our cause.

Of course the first presentation was the one which caused most nerves, for me at least, not knowing quite what to expect. Fortunately and fortuitously the young fund manager, capable of signing up for several million pounds worth of stock, turned out to be a relatively recent Brasenose engineering graduate, so we did not feel intimidated. We explained that we were selling about one-third of the company which would capitalise the newly named Oxford Molecular Group Plc at about £30 million.

Our spirits went up and down as we discussed whether our shows had the desired effect. Obviously the market was getting less and less receptive to new issues. We spoke to fund managers who had already seen perhaps thirty presentations that month. Real jitters started when we learned that Cortecs, the company that was one ahead of us in the Henry Cooke pipeline, was having its launch delayed. They were revived when Richard Lucas was able to tell us that some promises were coming in.

The final day of our performances was much like the first. We were exhausted with the effort, not just of dashing around, but also because of the strain in trying to sound fresh and exciting with the same material that had been used thirty times before. Happily the last presentation, which was to M & G, was attended by a fund manager who turned out to be another old friend, Jonathan Bartlett. Jonathan had been a junior Research Fellow at Brasenose, then a tutor in French at St Anne's College, Oxford, where he transformed Oxford University rugby football before joining the City. We were able to return to Oxford on the train together and learn some of the intricacies of the current state of the market from him.

It was clear that the window of opportunity for new issues was closing rapidly as the market drifted downwards. Thus it was a matter of relief as well as pleasure when we learned from Henry Cooke that in the jargon of the City "we had got it away" – the funds for which we were asking had been forthcoming at a price of 72p per share. When that price had been fixed we had been mildly disappointed, hoping for perhaps 75p. In the event we were very happy with it and felt that the advice had been good.

In addition to convincing the City fund managers, we also of course needed to make an impact on the share buying public. This involved hiring a City public relations team in addition to Andrew Lloyd who remained with us acting largely in the technical area. He organised a day with technical journals and broadcasters and on that side we were well served. The general public relations pieces in the national press and quality Sunday papers also looked good, but this was more due to our own efforts rather than those of the professionals. Being associated with Oxford University and, what is more, the first company to be spun out of that ancient seat of learning, made for a good story. In *The Sunday Times Magazine* Tony and I were described as the biggest benefactors of Oxford University since Henry VIII. Given that even after the flotation the university would own almost 10% of the company, this statement is close to the truth, especially as the university disposed of most of its shares at £3.20 each. It is my view that universities ought always to sell a large proportion of their shares at the earliest opportunity.

Successful Flotation

With the roadshow over and the promises of support in, there was a period of calm for a few days until dealing started. That day was a real reward: less than five years from starting out Oxford Molecular Group Plc appeared on the screens as a traded stock with the initial price achieving a satisfactory premium over the issue price. It was a time for celebration – champagne, a dinner from Barclays Bank in their directors' dining room, and above all the satisfactory feeling of having £9 million in the bank, our advisors having charged us £1 million.

We also had one final lunch of the old Oxford Molecular Ltd board and venture capital observers. This was held in the Bear at Woodstock with the arrangements being largely the work of Paul Bailey. To our surprise he himself did not turn up at the very jovial function. Even more upsetting was his subsequent suicide. We all felt we had lost a good friend and someone who had made enormous contributions to getting the company into existence and to the process of becoming a Plc. The next step would be to use the money from the flotation wisely, expanding into the USA and developing our contract design business.

Acquisition Of IntelliGenetics

In late 1993, before we had even made the decision to go for a public offering, Tony had been in discussion with the US oil giant Amoco about their wholly owned subsidiary IntelliGenetics Inc. Once again this opportunity arose from a question of ripe time. In the 1980s, major corporations such as oil companies diversified madly. The fashion was to get into new promising areas, particularly those involved in high technology, so as to build a long-term future for that unquantifiable time when the oil "runs out". The slogan of the 1990s, by contrast was "back to basics" or "concentrate on the core business".

It was with this background that Tony became aware that Amoco might be interested in selling IntelliGenetics Inc. Their area of business was one into which we had for a long time wanted to expand, bioinformatics – based on gene sequences – the ideal compliment to our own area of expertise with proteins and small molecules. Our long-term objective had been, and remained, to cover the entire science of drug discovery from the gene, via protein, to small molecule drugs. Discussions with one small US company, GCG Wisconsin, had been held to see if a marriage was possible, but they preferred independence at that time.

The chance to make a liaison with IntelliGenetics was just what Oxford Molecular needed. They had a similar background to us and had complementary technology. IntelliGenetics had been founded in 1980 by four Stanford academics, Douglas Brutlag being principal among them, and he had remained a consultant to the company. They had been supported by venture capital to the tune of some $3 million until making an initial public offering in 1983, which raised a further $8.8 million. In 1986 a joint venture was formed by the company and Amoco with the oil company holding 60% of the shares, and then in 1990 IntelliGenetics became a wholly-owned subsidiary of Amoco Technology.

In 1997 IntelliGenetics won a five year $22 million contract to improve, maintain and distribute US National DNA Sequence Databank ("GenBank"), but in 1992 the contract to continue this distribution was taken up by the National Center for Biological Information, a division of the US National Library of Medicine. The company had subsequently slipped back somewhat, despite being at the time the world's largest seller of genetics software. It was with this background that Tony entered into negotiations with Bob DePaul of Amoco in late 1993. The primary difficulty was the thought of trying to set up a major merger or acquisition whilst at the same time undergoing a flotation. It was just not humanly possible, even for Tony, so the matter was put on hold until the completion of our initial public offering.

Hence it was almost immediately, following Oxford Molecular's successful launch on the Stock Exchange, that negotiations were resumed. One complicating feature became apparent almost immediately. The sales of IntelliGenetics were larger than those of Oxford Molecular so that, in the eyes of the regulators of the London Stock Exchange, we were going to be involved in a reverse takeover. The significance of this was that it once again necessitated producing an entire prospectus, with all the work that this entailed, including audits of both companies and a long-form report – a very profitable process for our lawyers and bankers.

Despite the pressure the acquisition was completed by September 1994 for an aggregate consideration of $5.2 million, largely in shares in Oxford Molecular Group, with Amoco like the earlier investors being locked in for two years.

The intellectual property that came with the deal gave us what we sought: software to analyse DNA sequences. The software worked on Apple Mac machines and personal computers as well as on workstations. In addition it included a system for massively parallel computers developed in pioneering work by John Collins at Edinburgh University. Thus we were expanding our academic network as well as getting seriously involved in the all-important US market.

As in any takeover there were also difficult decisions about personnel. Who should go and who should stay so that there were savings gained from the merger, but not to the extent of emasculating the combined company? We gained some superb sales people who had done particularly well in Europe, but saw the chief area where savings could be made as being on the technical side, since programmers were less expensive in the UK than in the US. Shedding people is never easy and probably particularly difficult in small companies where everyone knows everyone else. In the USA one has to be particularly careful so as to avoid being sued. Some of the departing female employees did suggest they would hire lawyers to allege sexual harassment but as it turned out this threat did not materialise. By the end of 1994 the IntelliGenetics division of Oxford Molecular was slimmed down, on budget and making major contributions to the whole company, while we had kept one of the major promises in the flotation prospectus – expansion into the US market.

Not only was the input from IntelliGenetics important from a commercial point of view, perhaps more significantly it gave us a major presence in the area of genetics, which is without doubt the front-runner among all current scientific disciplines. Billions of dollars were being spent worldwide in the Human Genome Project to sequence the entire human genome. If this vast amount of data is to be useful it has to be organised and searched with computational tools. In Britain it is an area of science in which we excel, in no small part due to the support given by the Wellcome Trust. At Hinxton Hall, near Cambridge, the Trust, with a little help from the Medical Research Council, has invested many millions in sequencing. In Oxford they supported the Nuffield Professor of Medicine, John Bell, to the tune of some £25 million to study human genetics and multigene problems such as diabetes. It was into this area that we wanted to grow and to use our previous software products to go to small molecule products for the pharmaceutical industry. We thus felt it important to include John Bell in our plans as an advisor, particularly as his group is one of the world leaders in bioinformatics.

A major coup in the same vein was the agreement of James Watson (of Watson and Crick fame) to join our International Scientific Advisory Panel. This was no mere tokenism. During the academic year 1993-94, Jim was in Oxford as the Newton-Abraham visiting professor. Hence it was possible to see a lot of him and to get his advice. An unexpected bonus from the acquisition was the purchase of a very complete set of gymnasium equipment since the Palo Alto company had its own gym. We were not able to transfer this to the new premises so we sent the equipment in a container to Oxford, along with their impressive boardroom table. The gym was set up in the Oxford offices and a personal trainer was hired, allowing all employees time off during work periods to use the facility. This was a wonderful corporate move. Some 80% of the employees took advantage of the equipment and it did prove a channel for people in different parts of the company and at different levels to meet and interact. The one person who did not use the gym was the one person who needed it most; Tony.

Acquisition Of CAChe

Flotation and an acquisition all in one year is quite a mouthful for a small company, but it was not by any means the whole story. Yet another takeover possibility was suggested by Tony – it had occurred to him as a result of his talking with other companies in the field. The takeover candidate was CAChe Scientific Inc. The name derives from Computer-Aided Chemistry and the background was remarkably similar to our opportunity with IntelliGenetics.

CAChe was based in Beaverton, near Portland, Oregon, and had been founded in 1986 within a research division of the major corporation Tektronix, best known as a maker of scientific electronic instrumentation. Again this was the period where corporations expanded into novel high technology growth areas. CAChe was formed as a subsidiary of Tektronix in November 1991 and in 1993, Sony and Tektronix subscribed to 30% of the company's equity for $105 million in a joint venture. This investment was to be used for product development. Perhaps as a result of this link with Sony, CAChe had the largest part of the Japanese market for computer-aided design software. They also had a joint development agreement with the scientific and technical application software unit of IBM's Research Centre at Almaden, California.

From the viewpoint of Oxford Molecular, the really attractive feature of the CAChe company was the quality of their computer interfaces and above all the magnificent display of molecules on the screen. Without doubt the visual quality of their software was second to none – it allowed not just simple representation of molecules, but also molecular motion and three-dimensional viewing. In terms of the front end, which a working chemist or student would see, they were in a class of their own. Conversely, if we were to be critical, what they seemed to lack was much hard science behind the interface. This was the complete reverse of our own situation so there seemed to be a chance of a happy marriage.

One of our visions, slowly becoming fact, was that bench chemists, who make molecules in pharmaceutical and biotechnology research laboratories, increasingly used computers for themselves – they did not merely go down the corridor to consult the resident expert. This being so, there was an absolute need for systems that would work on Apple Macintosh or personal computers with simple looking but sophisticated interfaces. These were the strengths of CAChe.

By now a veteran of takeovers, Tony, together with Rod Hall and Christopher Weston, proceeded very quickly with the negotiations with Tektronix. This time round we were not involved in a reverse takeover, just the common or garden variety. Audits had to be made of both companies, but of course whereas buying a small independent company might be difficult from an auditing point of view, buying from a major corporation essentially ensures that there are no hidden pitfalls in the books.

Only in one tiny area did a conflict between our lawyers and theirs fail to be resolved instantly. Tektronix had moved CAChe to a new business park on what had been an industrial site. Our lawyers saw it as imperative for us to have absolute protection against any claims to be made at some future date in respect of pollution or environmental effects dating back to events that would have taken place years before we had any connection with the site. One only wishes that the lawyers working for Lloyd's of London had been as scrupulous, in which case many names would not have fared so badly.

The negotiations were all but complete by Christmas 1994 with the loose ends tied up by January. The final low hurdle, required by Stock

Exchange regulations, was an extraordinary general meeting of the company so that shareholders could attend to vote on the change in the company if they so wished. Prior to this, of course, each of our 3,000 or so shareholders had received listing particulars of the issuing of new shares that were to be used for the purchase. Our major shareholders were visited and had the details of the transaction and the scientific and commercial rationale explained.

The only question raised at the EGM was the same as had been put on the occasion of the IntelliGenetics merger: why should a small loss-making company buy another company in a similar position? The answer was obvious and universally accepted. It encompassed, above all, the further shift of the centre of gravity of the company towards the USA and a huge lift in our prospects in Japan. Oxford Molecular had been strong in Europe but weak in the USA. CAChe was in the converse position. The combination was clearly going to benefit both companies. The takeover was agreed with Oxford Molecular, buying with our own shares. Everything was complete by 1995.

After rationalisation, as the distressing business of letting some employees go is called, the company's workforce was just over a hundred people with headquarters in the Oxford Science Park and with development, sales and administration offices at Mountain View in California and Beaverton, Oregon. Additional sales offices were located on the campus of the École Polytechnique in Paris and at the University of Erlangen-Nürnberg in Germany. The Japanese market was served by the partners of the three combined companies Sony/Tek, Toray Systems Centre and Teijin.

By the end of 1995 at least three major collaborations were announced: with the then Glaxo Wellcome to provide desktop solutions for their medicinal chemists; with Applied Biosystems to provide our data-handling software on their new generation of DNA sequencers; and with Silicon Graphics Inc, who at that time had virtually the entire market for computer hardware in the area of drug design.

Acquisition Of MacVector And Health Designs

The acquisition fever also continued. The bioinformatics software named MacVector was purchased from Eastman Kodak. The computer-aided toxicology business Health Designs Inc based in Rochester, New York, where the leading scientist involved was yet another former "postdoc" of mine, Vijay Gombar, was also acquired.

The End Of The Lock-In

Not surprisingly the City loved this activity and for two consecutive years we were amongst the fastest rising shares on the London Stock Exchange. The rapid growth persuaded us that we needed more heavyweight advisors and we were taken on by Cazenove, one of the City's most prestigious banks. We were later to learn that they could be just as hard and avaricious as any barrow boy, but they did do some remarkable things for us. Most notably when the two-year lock-in period following the IPO came to an end they handled brilliantly what could have been a very difficult time. When the original shareholders became free to sell their shares, some 60% of the company was suddenly saleable. This included the university and the venture capitalists as well as the founders. Cazenove were brilliant in the sense that through a period when one might have expected the share price to fall, it in fact just rose smoothly, onward and upward.

Cazenove proved outstanding at placing the shares amongst their friends, although the all-important selling roadshow was again performed by Tony and, to a lesser extent, by me. This in fact left a slightly sour taste, since having done most of the work Tony and I were telephoned on the final evening and told, contrary to what we had been promised, that we could only sell one-third of our shares rather than one-half. For me this was an irritation as I felt we had been conned, but for Tony it was more serious as he had already spent the promised cash on a farm, which he later sold at a profit. In addition, and more sensationally, he had splashed out on the famous steam locomotive the Flying Scotsman and its carriages – a saga which is well worth another book.

Sex

One unforeseen problem in the thriving company was sex. Nearly all our employees were in their 20s or early 30s, with a near equal number of male and female employees. Hormone levels were dangerously high and we had a number of problematic relationships that resulted in us losing some otherwise excellent employees. Even if people had important talents we could not countenance someone spending much of the working day sending mildly pornographic emails to someone on the other side of the room. Even our gym failed to divert some people's energy.

Contract Design

Another new strategy, which became possible after flotation, was to use our own software and carefully nurtured academic contacts to do contract design. To a small extent this strategy was already being followed prior to the initial public offering. Antibody modelling contracts were completed successfully by Tony Rees and his group at Bath for NeoRx and for Immunogen. These contracts involved the humanisation of antibodies, that is changing the make-up of an antibody raised in a mouse so that it is seen as of human origin by the human immune system. This type of contract can bring in sums of the order of a few hundred thousand dollars. What we were more interested in were contracts worth several millions of dollars with major pharmaceutical companies.

At first sight it may seem strange that a pharmaceutical company with a research budget of hundreds of millions of dollars per year might contemplate outsourcing some of its fundamental research. However, the time was certainly ripe for this to happen and a number of small companies succeeded in winning significant contracts.

One reason why this was starting to happen was the radical restructuring of the drug industry. As we had foreseen, the situation where the biggest companies in a major industry only have less than 5% each of the market and also do the complete job from top to bottom – research, development, marketing and selling – was not likely to last. As became obvious, there would be mergers and takeovers so that the top players have nearer 20% of the market share: Bristol Myers and Squibb, SmithKline and French with Beecham, Glaxo with Wellcome. Many more followed and continue to this day.

Even the very big merged companies with enormous research departments can only cover a range of perhaps a dozen therapeutic goals. They are the sort of large organisation that is brilliant at development, but less well geared towards completely new lines of research. For a major company to get involved with a risky new area may involve building new laboratories, certainly hiring new staff with special expertise and creating something that it is difficult to wind up. If the project is done outside, provided strict confidentiality can be ensured, then only a fixed fee is risked, and the outcome should be novel lead compounds, which the big company can develop and market.

The best new ideas often originate in academic laboratories, but these are not ideal for commercial research as confidentiality is difficult and academic researchers have other priorities beyond making profits. This is the case even though academics and their departments are anything but naive with respect to funding.

What is needed is a middleman, and Oxford Molecular was in an ideal position to fulfil this role, having its spectacular list of academic partners, which included three Nobel Laureates. Indeed, it was almost a virtual pharmaceutical company.

The outline is perhaps obvious and the opportunities enormous. To get such a notion off the ground, however, requires a tangible project that can be sold to research directors. A mere idea is not enough. Major companies may receive hundreds of speculative ideas from academics who all believe that their particular project will generate enormous amounts of cash for the company and themselves, but companies just cannot in general take up lots of new ideas, however attractive. Far more likely to succeed are ideas supported by a business plan based on sound finance, which can be presented as a possible deal.

The Chloride Channel Project

The first such proposal from Oxford Molecular was put together by Roland Kozlowski of the university's Department of Pharmacology. It concerned channels in cell membranes through which chloride ions are passed. This was an ideal topic since chloride channels were not current targets, even though similar channels which transport calcium ions or potassium ions are the object of massive research, with blockers of those channels providing markets of many billions of dollars, particularly in the area of cardiovascular and heart disease.

Chloride channels are implicated in therapeutic areas, which include asthma, cardiac arrhythmias, cystic fibrosis and eye cataracts. The combined area was thought to have a market value of maybe $20 billion. Roland put together a scientific team under a steering committee chaired by the recently retired Master of Balliol College and Nobel prize-winner, Baruch Blumberg. The team included Professor Christopher Higgins, then head of the Nuffield Department of Clinical Biochemistry and an expert in the molecular biology of chloride channels. His role was to produce sequences of the channels, which would be modelled by my group, and then make mutants to test whether the models explain the experimental facts. Based on the structure of the channel and some known rather poor inhibitors, Steve Davies of Oxford's Organic Chemistry Laboratory, and himself the scientific founder of Oxford Asymmetry, would synthesise novel compounds. The effects of these compounds would be tested by Kieran Kirk of the Physiology Laboratory using electrophysiological techniques, and by Roland himself.

The project was specifically designed to complement, and not to compete with, in-house research. It enabled the investing company to gain a fundamental assessment of the chloride channel as a target for drugs in a highly effective way. That specific proposal was put to some 32 major pharmaceutical companies across the world, in Japan as well as in Europe and the USA. The final deal was struck with Yamanouchi of Japan who proved excellent partners in a successful three-year £10 million project.

Further Acquisitions

Further acquisitions included the vitally important cheminformatics division of PSI International in Baltimore funded by a successful rights issue in 1996. By this stage the company had the nearly complete range of software products required for drug discovery: genetics software, protein modelling and cheminformatics, and small molecule products. We even finally added GCG Wisconsin, the world's premier bioinformatics group, to the family. It was impressive albeit stretching, with some seven separate active sites in the US alone.

Cambridge Discovery Chemistry

This rapid growth was, however, not enough to satisfy our vision or our ambitions. We conceived of the drug discovery process as having three legs: the computational side, where we were becoming pre-eminent; the synthesis of drug candidate molecules, at that time most fashionably using combinatorial methods; and third their screening, preferably using high throughput techniques involving robots. Being a listed company imposed constraints. If we had just invested in these areas our profitability would have been damaged and delayed. The only way to avoid having the initial years of new ventures leaving their results consolidated into those of the main company was to set up new ventures, using our cash, but owning less than the legal limit of 20% of the new ventures. In this way we founded Cambridge Combinatorial Ltd, bringing in the Cambridge academics Steve Ley and Alan Fersht, but with Tony's younger brother Allan as CEO from Pfizer, where he had been a medicinal chemist for some years. In a similar way the screening company Cambridge Drug Discovery was set up with another former Pfizer scientist, Mark Treherne, as the managing director.

Cambridge Drug Discovery was fairly quickly sold to Cambridge Genetics Ltd, but Cambridge Combinatorial, renamed as Cambridge Discovery Chemistry, was such a quick success, thanks largely to Allan's skill, that it posed a problem. Oxford Molecular had an agreement with the shareholders of the 80% of the company that we did not own to buy them out according to a formula based on sales during their first three years of operation. This formula was not very clear and the board was suffering from poor financial information. The success of Cambridge Discovery Chemistry meant that we had to buy them out very quickly at a very high price. As a result Allan Marchington made a very rapid large profit that was misunderstood and badly received by a hostile City. They imagined that there had been a deep-seated plot by one Marchington brother to put money into the pocket of the other. Almost over night we passed from being the darlings of the City, which had made many millions from us, into pariahs who were not to be supported. It was the beginning of a sad end to what had hitherto been a spectacular success story.

The Demise Of The Company

Just at the point where we had completed the grand design for the company with "design, make and test", all in one group of companies, the bottom fell out of biotech stocks with our share price tumbling from 400p in May 1997 to 80p in December of that year, despite revenues increasing from £15 million to £22 million. By the spring of 1999 Cazenove, our brokers, strongly urged that a new board was essential. Douglas Brown, a former Barings director, was brought in as chairman, and Laurence Steingold became a new finance director.

Tony's response to the pressures and an increasingly hostile board was to propose a management buy-out for which it was clear that financial backing was available. The board would however not countenance such a move and total mistrust and acrimony ensued. Inevitably under such conditions things could not go on. Subsequent to my own resignation, the company entered a Members' Voluntary Liquidation in September

2000 with the Discovery Chemistry business being sold to Millennium Pharmaceuticals, and the Software Division to Pharmacopeia Inc, later to be renamed Accelrys Inc. It is probably true that we made a classic error in keeping Tony as the CEO long after our IPO. A very different animal is required to run a big company with hundreds of employees in a multinational context from the man or woman capable of taking a company from nothing to flotation. Tony was a genius at the latter, but probably not the ideal man to run the established entity. He should have left with a large sum of money and repeated the start-up phase many times.

The highlights of the Oxford Molecular story include having 25% of the world bioinformatics market, the biggest share of the Japanese modelling market and 60% of sales in the USA. We had 400 employees with half being in the US. Oxford University received £10 million.

All of the company is now foreign owned and has proved to have real value. The same is true of other Oxford spin-out successes. A company in the United States owns Powderject and Oxford Asymmetry is now German. It does seem to be a depressing feature of UK academic spin-outs that we are getting good at creating the £100 million company, but are not patient enough to grow £1 billion companies.

7

Wider University Coverage – IP Group Plc

Funding A New Chemistry Laboratory

The biggest task during my tenure as the Chairman of Oxford University's Chemistry Department was to build a new research laboratory. The department is the biggest in the Western world, but by the 1990s some of its laboratories were barely fit for the purpose and not up to current health and safety standards. The cost was the main impediment: at least £50 million would be required. This type of problem was widespread in Britain where many of the university facilities, created in the 1960s, were getting very tired, and our organic chemistry labs included parts dating back to the early part of the twentieth century.

In response to this need the UK Government, together with The Wellcome Trust, set up a generous and imaginative scheme, the Joint Infrastructure Fund (JIF), to which one could make bids for funding projects, especially buildings. We were fortunate enough to receive the largest award given under the scheme, some £30 million. A further £9 million was secured from the Government's university funding council, and several million more from charities. British industry contributed £250,000, a generous donation from Thomas Swan Ltd.

The final detailed plans for what we intended to be the best possible laboratory were costed at over £60 million, leaving a funding gap of about £20 million. It fell to me to find this sum.

The Beeson-Gregory Deal

In that period, before the dotcom bubble burst, it is now hard to comprehend, but business angels and finance groups were almost desperate to fund high-tech companies. In Oxford the London group IndexIT, founded by David Norwood, had been the investor in a number of spin-outs, and with the help of Melissa Levitt of the university's Development Office, we made an approach to him seeking funding. David is a man of remarkable talent. He is an international chess grandmaster, and at about the time we started talking he sold his company to the ambitious London stockbroking firm of Beeson Gregory. In the spring of 2000 Beeson Gregory had a successful flotation which left them with a significant amount of cash in the bank, so our discussions with David and his colleagues became serious.

The initial suggestion from the Beeson Gregory side was for them to put up a sum of cash in return for the right to be the investor in spin-out companies emanating from the Chemistry Department. Unfortunately this was something I could not sell. The key step in founding a spin-out is the three way meeting involving the sponsors who provide the cash, the university that will be putting in the intellectual property, usually by means of a licence, and the academic involved, without whom the project cannot proceed. As explained earlier, the equity is then split into a compromise between the backers, the university and the academic or academics. If one party had the right to be the investor there would be no rational way of fixing the valuation or the relative shares. In addition, I could not commit my colleagues to receiving funding from one preferred or monopoly source. It was possible that some of us who had previously successful ventures might like to use our own money or, more likely, to remain with the sponsors who had supported the previous company.

The alternative, cooked up between us, was for Beeson Gregory to provide an upfront sum in return for a percentage of the university equity in all chemistry spin-outs for a defined period of time. The three parameters in the potential funding deal were thus the sum of money provided, the percentage of equity going to Beeson Gregory, and the length of time the agreement would run. My opening gambit, nervous since I was playing with a master chess player, was to suggest £10 million for one-third of the university equity and a ten year deal. In the end we settled for £20 million for half the university equity over a fifteen year period. It must be remembered that this arrangement was fixed within weeks of the high point of the stock market, just before the crash. Even without the benefit of hindsight the deal has delivered significant financial benefit to the university, allowed the completion of a magnificent laboratory, and established it as the flagship commercialisation partnership in Europe.

At the time, however, this was far from obvious and indeed it proved anything but easy to get this draft possibility accepted by the respective parent bodies. The initial reaction from the university was almost hostile. Phrases like "selling the family silver", were bandied about and there was much angst about how the figures had been arrived at. The bank, I believe, looked at our track record, Medisense, Oxford Molecular, and Oxford Asymmetry, all spin-outs from the Chemistry Department. In the case of the latter pair, very successful IPOs had been achieved so that had the deal been done some six years earlier it would have been very profitable to Beeson Gregory. They also discussed the possibility of future spin-outs and were encouraged by what they saw. From my naive point of view £20 million over fifteen years for a venture capitalist would require perhaps a 20% annual return. If Beeson Gregory only owned 12%, half a typical university share in each company, then the market capitalisation of spun-out companies at the end of the period would have to run into billions for them to make significant returns. It had to be remembered, however, that although they had no right to be the supplier of capital, Beeson Gregory could nevertheless be so, and were likely to be in a strong position to know what was going on in the department to assist in decision making. Thus it was a possibility that Beeson Gregory could hold perhaps half of a spin-out. In some ways the real beauty of the deal was and is that once a company is formed, the interests of the bank and the university are identical: the more the spin-out company prospers the better for both. It is not the case that the more one party makes, the less the other receives.

On the university side, selling this deal was resolved by the Registrar, David Holmes, who had the courage to say: 'We must do it.' This was despite the fact that something like this had never been done before, which is always a powerful counter argument in Oxford.

With Beeson Gregory the final hurdle was to convince their chairman Andrew Beeson, a goal which was achieved over a lunch in David Norwood's favourite Oxford restaurant. That meeting started rather tensely and I had the impression that things were not going as well as we had hoped, when one of those serendipitous events occurred which reinforce my belief in the cock-up theory of history. During the lunch Andrew asked if the tie that I happened to be wearing was the tie of Vincent's Club, an Oxford club largely devoted to sportsmen. I replied that it was indeed, and he enquired about my sporting interests. On returning the conversation he revealed that he was a keen, indeed high-class player of real tennis, the ancient original tennis game with complex rules and scoring, played on indoor courts. I then asked if he had come across one of my chemistry pupils, Spike Willcocks, who was a notable university player. Suddenly there was a change of mood – all smiles as he knew and admired Spike and the deal was agreed. Subsequently Spike joined Beeson Gregory and its successor IP2IPO where his talent was a significant bonus on top of the funding deal.

Having the arrangement for funding agreed at the heads of terms level, we then brought in the lawyers, but most issues were readily soluble. The same arrangements were to apply to licensing agreements as to spin-outs: Beeson Gregory would receive half of what the university would have got. More problematic was defining who exactly was included amongst the academics as a chemist. Fortunately we had a simple and clear-cut definition provided by the government's Research Assessment Exercise (the RAE), where all academics are entered under a particular unit of assessment, one of which is Chemistry. There is no way the department would want to cheat by redefining one of the members of staff as, say, a biochemist, since that would cost us funding. Any work done by someone defined as a chemist in this way is included, even if the actual research was done outside our labs, in Grenoble for example. Similarly, work done in our chemistry laboratories by outsiders who come in, perhaps to use some of our equipment, is excluded. It was also agreed that if a spin-out involved work of perhaps a chemist and an engineer, the academics could decide on the split between themselves, and this would determine how much of the input was from Chemistry and thus the Beeson Gregory percentage. In practice the academics have normally agreed equal shares.

Since the deal was with a public company it was a price sensitive issue and had to be conducted as a matter of secrecy. This meant that I could not consult my departmental colleagues and the wider university until the deal was formally announced. An email to all the faculty on the morning of the announcement explained the details of the arrangement and tried to answer the obvious questions, but we also had weekly lunches with the academics – four at a time – involving Beeson Gregory and Isis Innovation, the university technology transfer company. This gave the opportunity to ask questions, to understand the details and, most usefully, to explore the intellectual property opportunities, both existing patents taken out by Isis and ideas in the pipeline.

It was important for my academic colleagues, and indeed the outside world, to understand that we had not sold forward any intellectual property. The IP is owned by the university and would be licensed into the spin-outs, with it being returned were the company to fail. They also had to be reassured that their own rights and share of the equity in a spin-out are not affected, only the university portion. The real bonuses, however, were the input from Beeson Gregory in preparing business plans, the use of their analysts and, most importantly, particularly following the sudden loss of confidence in the stock market, in the raising of funds. During a period when finding the cash to launch spin-outs became almost impossible since they are too small for venture capitalists, the Beeson Gregory people, notably David Norwood, came up with the funding for some of the nine new companies from the department in the first four years of the deal.

Inhibox Ltd

The first of these new spin-out companies, Inhibox, was derived from my own academic research. I have led a reasonably successful career based in part on picking up ideas from other fields and adapting them to my own problems. The scientific side of Inhibox goes back to the brilliant idea of some Berkeley scientists who conceived the SETI project. SETI is an acronym for Search for Extraterrestrial Intelligence. NASA, the US space agency, records the radio signals that arrive on Earth at all times and from all directions. A piece of relatively simple computer code can analyse a signal to ascertain whether it is an intelligent signal rather than just noise, but since there are so many individual signals to process the only way to do this is to use a lot of small computers rather than a few big machines. The Berkeley group hit on the notion of getting the analysis software into a screensaver for use on home computers, and then issuing signals to analyse over the Internet. It is a brilliant idea and has come to involve over five million

PCs. On the other hand this research has not produced a scientific result – ET has not yet been found to have rung in – but as a computational idea and to compare the speeds of different PCs it is not without value.

Some of the people associated with the project established the start-up company United Devices in Austin, Texas, to try to exploit the idea. In order to gain publicity and help raise funding they offered to run three pro bono projects and invited ideas, in space science, environmental science, and in health science. Much of my own research is financed by a US cancer charity, the National Foundation for Cancer Research (NFCR). With their encouragement I came up with the idea that we could adapt the SETI idea to look for potential anti-cancer drugs: doing essentially the same type of research done in pharmaceutical companies, but on a larger scale. Drugs are usually little molecules that work by binding to a specific target site on a protein and interfere with its action. Many protein targets are known and in the future many more are certain to be identified. Our idea was thus very simple: build a database of as many small drug-like molecules as we could, making sure that they had appropriate properties and we knew how to synthesise them; identify target sites and have a quick piece of computer code to calculate just how well each small molecule can bind to the site; finally, wrap them up in a screensaver and use the Internet to send the input to those PCs across the world running the project.

My partner in this was Keith Davies, another former Oxford chemist who had been the founder of the company Chemical Design. United Devices provided the distributed computing, with the initial project being sponsored by Intel. The success of the venture was amazing. More than three million PCs signed up, providing in excess of 400,000 hours of CPU time, permitting 14 cancer targets to be screened and yielding many thousands of potential drug leads: a long way from a drug, but an important first step. The intellectual property derived from this much publicised project belonged to Oxford University, but to make use of it the obvious avenue was to create a new company, Inhibox. One sensitive issue was the disquiet amongst some of the generous folk, who contributed time on their PCs when not using the machines themselves, about this being exploited for commercial gain. Money has to be involved since following up the computer predictions with synthesis of the molecules and testing them is far from inexpensive. To allay the fears of the public the shares in the company that would have gone to me were donated to the NFCR so that a large part of the hoped-for financial success of the company will benefit the charity, which will in turn recycle the cash back into cancer research.

Further Spin-Outs

Other spin-out companies from the department encompassed by the deal, and for which funding was found in a difficult period, include Pharminox, based on the work of the late Gordon Lowe and a large class of platinum compounds, Zyentia, a platform technology concerned with protein folding and drug development derived from Chris Dobson's research, and Glycoform, drug delivery and carbohydrate work from Ben Davis and Antony Fairbanks. On the non life-science side Oxford Medical Diagnostics came from Gus Hancock's work in physical chemistry. That company later merged with Avacta Group Plc, the Leeds University spin-out.

Four of the department's spin-outs have already made significant progress, including three becoming Plcs, and ReOx, which found inhibitors for HIF (hypoxia inducible factor) through the work of Chris Schofield, obtained a multi-million pound contract with a major pharmaceutical company.

VastOx Ltd was founded in 2003 based on the work of Steve Davies. The company has expertise in carbohydrate chemistry, but most notably turns drug discovery on its head by using zebra fish embryos. Crudely, the modern form of the traditional drug discovery process involves having the target protein in solution in wells on a 96-well plate and having a robot add a different chemical molecule, the potential drug, to each well. One then seeks those compounds that bind most tightly to the target. In the VastOx case each well contains four cells of a zebra fish embryo and molecules are again added by a robot. One then seeks molecules which do something to the grown fish, that is have affected some target, and from a knowledge of the genetics of the zebra fish that target can be identified. If that proves to be an interesting target then one has an initial lead compound and, in addition, having been introduced into a vertebrate, one has some useful information about possible toxicological problems. The company had an IPO in October 2004 and, now renamed as Summit Corporation Plc, is a thriving small company with a market capitalisation of around £60 million.

Oxford Catalysts Group Plc came from work in inorganic chemistry conducted by Malcolm Green and Tiancun Xiao. They created novel catalysts that are carbides and can be used to generate superheated steam and hydrogen at room temperature. This work gives hope for the much desired energy solution of having a fuel cell driven by the reaction of the hydrogen with oxygen from the air to produce only energy and water. In the past the drawback to this notion has been storing the hydrogen. Their catalysts can also be used to clean up fossil fuels. The company had an IPO in 2006 and has a market capitalisation of some £60 million.

Oxford Advanced Surfaces Group Plc develops and commercialises advanced materials by modifying the surface properties with a range of applications – these include wetting properties, adhesion, metallisation and bioactivity. The company joined the Alternative Investment Market (AIM) by means of a reverse takeover of Kanyon Plc and now has a market capitalisation of £160 million.

Oxford Nanolabs, founded in 2005 and now renamed Oxford Nanopore Technologies Ltd, remains a private company but has received very significant funding and appears to have a very exciting future. Based on the research of Hagan Bayley, the company creates nanopores – small holes that may be adapted to detect different molecules – and is widely seen as the most likely contender to win the race to sequence the human genome, for as little as $1,000. They have recently concluded a collaboration with Harvard University and the University of Santa Cruz.

As far as Oxford has been concerned, the partnership started with Beeson Gregory has been wholly beneficial and much envied. The real importance, however, has been in the wider context since it led David Norwood to develop a new business model that has had a profound influence. A second university deal was made by David and his colleagues with the University of Southampton, but in that case it involved the entire university. Beeson Gregory did not provide an upfront sum, but rather bolstered the university technology transfer organisation by seconding a member of staff, and provided a £5 million fund to finance new spin-outs. This has been outstandingly successful with two of their spin-outs having had successful IPOs (OHM and SynAirgen) giving the university a multi-million pound return.

IP2IPO Group Plc

Beeson Gregory itself was merged with the Evolution Group, which set up a wholly owned subsidiary under the name IP2IPO – "intellectual property to initial public offering" – of which I became a non-executive director. In October 2003, IP2IPO was itself floated on the Alternative Investment Market, and became an independent company with Evolution subsequently disposing of all its shares by the spring of 2005.

In August 2004 I became chairman of IP2IPO Group Plc, by which time partnerships had been extended to include, as well as Oxford Chemistry and the University of Southampton, King's College London with its major medical school and hospitals. The partnership with King's is on the same lines as that with Southampton. IP2IPO is entitled to 20% of the university's interest in spin-out companies based on IP created across the entire university for 25 years, and has set up a fund to provide seed capital for which it can receive additional equity if it invests. This arrangement makes it important for IP2IPO to assist in every way – helping with business plans, raising capital, and above all finding management, which is perhaps still the most significant bottleneck in the UK.

A fourth partnership involved the University of York. Their go-ahead vice-chancellor, Brian Cantor, was previously the head of the Mathematical and Physical Sciences Division at Oxford and thus familiar with, and attracted by, the idea of a partnership. With his support IP2IPO acquired a one-third interest in Amaethon Ltd, a company that had been formed to commercialise the IP created in the university's plant genomics department – the Centre for Novel Agricultural Products. Again, IP2IPO provides the seed capital to spin-out companies created by Amaethon.

The University of Leeds, as we have seen, quite independently adopted a somewhat different path for the commercialisation of its science. In their case the role played in Oxford by Isis was outsourced to an independent company, Techtran Group Limited. Techtran were set up by Axiomlab Group Plc in 2002 to offer commercialisation services to research intensive institutions. They had their own team, led by Alan Aubrey and Alison Fielding, which includes people with backgrounds not just in science, but also corporate finance and management consulting. This team, being part of a commercial organisation, is better equipped than are the vast majority of technology transfer offices. The Techtran model has proved to be very successful with more than 20 companies having been created, of which four have become successful public companies either by IPOs or by reverse takeovers.

This interesting approach commended itself to IP2IPO, which first bought a 20% stake in Techtran with David Norwood becoming a director. Then, liking what he saw, IP2IPO acquired the Techtran group in January 2005, with Alan becoming CEO of IP2IPO and Alison the technical director of IP Group.

The annual report of IP2IPO for the year ending December 2004 showed a spectacular set of successes. Highlights of the report included the successful flotation of three companies, realisation of nearly £1 million from the sale of shares in a spin-out company, Offshore Hydrocarbon Mapping (OHM) from Southampton, and a market value of shares in quoted companies of £24 million. The company traded profitably and had over £30 million cash.

It is interesting to note that still the most productive and profitable part of the IP Group portfolio remains the original Oxford Chemistry deal, which has become established as the flagship commercialisation partnership in Europe and enabled the Group to become the leading European IP specialist.

Other Entrants To The Space

Not surprisingly this achievement has played a significant role in encouraging other companies and universities to enter into the space of exploitation of academic intellectual property.

Another entrant into the world of university IP and its exploitation with a novel variant is BioFusion, now Fusion IP Plc. This is an AIM listed company which raised over £8 million in the spring of 2005 essentially to exploit the medical research of the University of Sheffield, with whom it has a ten-year agreement. This really amounts to privatising the university technology transfer office for their defined category of intellectual property. Their basic idea is that the university concentrates on creating intellectual property while the company focuses on exploitation, having funds available to facilitate this. The university is a shareholder in the company. They have recently added an arrangement with the University of Wales, Cardiff.

A similar model has been followed by Imperial College, which in 2005 placed shares in its technology transfer organisation, Imperial College Ventures, and subsequently had a successful IPO as Imperial Innovations. Other new entrants include Sigma, which has partnerships with Dundee and Robert Gordon, Angle, partnered with Reading, and IPSO, which is linked to Loughborough. MTI have launched a fund focused on Manchester. The European Investment Fund has launched a Technology Transfer Accelerator Programme that has led to investments in IP Venture Fund, Leuven and the Manchester Fund.

IP Group Plc

In June 2006, IP2IPO, having changed its name to IP Group Plc, moved from AIM to a listing on the main board of the London Stock

Exchange. Particularly in the recent period when raising funds for start-up companies has proved problematic, the group has developed a strategy whereby it uses its own funds to help create "incubation businesses" before raising the extra money to turn the successful small companies, referred to as "grubs", into fully fledged entities. Formal deals now exist with the universities of Bath, Bristol, King's College London, York, Southampton, Surrey, Queen Mary College London and Glasgow, as well as Leeds and Oxford.

Table 7 lists the companies created by the group, excluding a large number of incubation businesses, together with some valuations (taken in the summer of 2008).

Company name	Description of business	Group Stake 30 Jun 2008	Fair value of holding 30 June 2008
Activotec SPP Limited	Supplier of chemical technology products for the pharma and biotech industry. Focused on peptide/protein synthesis technologies	35.3%	<£1.0m
Amaethon Limited	IP commercialisation of plant and microbial science	33.0%	<£1.0m
Apex Optoelectronics Limited	Growth of materials and epistructures based on free standing III-V nitride compound semi-conductors including (without limitation) free standing gallium nitride materials	5.5%	<£0.5m
Avacta Group plc	Advanced molecular detection and analysis technologies for the biopharmaceutical, homeland security, defence and medical diagnostics industries	23.9%	>£3.0m
Bioniqs Limited	Development of ionic liquids	30.1%	<£1.0m
Capsant Neurotechnologies Limited	Drug screening tools on ex vivo re-aggregated tissue	40.2%	<£0.5m
Chamelic Limited	Modification of surface reactions to external stimuli	46.4%	<£1.0m
COE Group plc	CCTV and surveillance technology	25.9%	<£3.0m

Company name	Description of business	Group Stake 30 Jun 2008	Fair value of holding 30 June 2008
Crysalin Limited	Developing crysalin lattice technology, a new area of protein-based nanotechnology	37.1%	<£0.5m
Dispersia Limited	Formulation of nanofluids for heat transfer applications	42.8%	<£0.5m
EMDOT Limited	Revolutionary electrostatic inkjet technology	24.6%	<£0.5m
GETECH Group plc	Gravity and magnetic data collection and interpretation services for oil, gas and mining industries	20.2%	<£3.0m
Glycoform Limited	Carbohydrate chemistry applied to protein drugs	9.7%	<£1.0m
Green Chemicals plc	Environmentally friendly textile and bleaching chemicals	24.5%	>£3.0m
Icona Solutions Limited	Software that enables engineers to see the impact of manufacturing variation of components on the finished assembly	49.9%	<£0.5m
Ilika Technologies Limited	Development and application of high throughput, combinatorial R&D techniques for the discovery of new materials	23.6%	>£3.0m
Inhibox Limited	Computational chemistry for screening lead candidates against targets	3.9%	<£0.5m
iQur Limited	Diagnosis and treatment of liver disorders	17.7%	>£3.0m
Karus Therapeutics Limited	Developing new drugs based on inhibitors of protein deacetylases	24.8%	<£0.5m
Leeds Lithium Power Limited	Lithium gel electrolyte plus manufacturing technologies	36.7%	<£0.5m
Leeds Reproductive Biosciences Limited	Viability of human eggs before fertilisation and re-implantation in IVF	43.8%	<£1.0m
Luto Research Limited	User testing of patient information leaflets	21.5%	<£0.5m
Modern Water plc	Water technologies to address problems of the availability of freshwater and the treatment and disposal of waste water	23.0%	>£3.0m

Company name	Description of business	Group Stake 30 Jun 2008	Fair value of holding 30 June 2008
Nanotecture Limited	Nanotechnology materials	10.2%	<£1.0m
Offshore Hydrocarbon Mapping plc	Electromagnetic methods of detecting offshore oil and gas reserves	0.8%	<£0.5m
Oxford Advanced Surfaces plc	Development and commercialisation of technology enabling modification of the surface properties of materials	15.7%	>£3.0m
Oxford Catalysts Group plc	Speciality catalysts for the generation of clean fuels, from both conventional fossil fuels and renewable sources such as biomass	16.7%	>£3.0m
Oxford Nanopore Technologies Limited	Diagnostic company developing highly innovative products for application in genomics, pharmacogenomics and high throughput drug discovery	34.9%	>£3.0m
Oxford RF Sensors Limited	Sensors to measure electromagnetic signature of materials to detect eg, position, wear, fluids etc.	22.9%	<£1.0m
OxTox Limited	Fast Marijuana Sensors	37.6%	<£0.5m
Perpetuum Limited	Micro Electrical Mechanical Systems (MEMS) to generate power from vibrational energy	8.2%	<£1.0m
Pharminox Limited	Cancer drug development	17.4%	<£3.0m
Photopharmica (Holdings) Limited	Develops novel photosensitisers as products for medical use & has opened up new applications of topical photodynamic therapy	49.9%	>£3.0m
Plexus Planning Limited	Project Management Software	29.3%	<£0.5m
Proximagen Neuroscience plc	Developing drugs for the treatment of neurodegenerative diseases	23.5%	>£3.0m
ReactivLab Limited	Company focusing on the diagnosis and prognosis of illness based on the analysis of specific biomarker proteins, notably the acute phase proteins	33.3%	<£0.5m

Company name	Description of business	Group Stake 30 Jun 2008	Fair value of holding 30 June 2008
ReOx Limited	Treating diseases by managing the body's response to oxygen using HIF	12.2%	<£0.5m
Retroscreen Virology Limited	CRO undertaking work on the preclinical / clinical screening of drugs to treat virus infection mainly flu	31.4%	<£3.0m
Revolymer Limited	Design, develops and formulates novel polymers that revolutionise consumer products. First application is removable "Clean Gum"	11.2%	>£3.0m
Rock Deformation Research Limited	Services and tools to examine impact of faults and other structures on hydrocarbon reserves	27.5%	<£0.5m
Sigma Technology Group plc	Early stage venture capital	4.0%	<£0.5m
Simulstrat Limited	War-gaming solutions for business	39.8%	<£0.5m
Stratophase Limited	Advanced opto-electric components	1.3%	<£0.5m
Structure Vision Limited	Particle packing software and technical consultancy	37.2%	<£1.0m
Summit Corporation plc	Using whole organism phenotypic screens for drug discovery and development	8.0%	<£3.0m
Surrey Nano Systems Limited	Silicon compatible machines and processes for growing nanostructures	40.0%	<£1.0m
Synairgen plc	Developing drugs for respiratory diseases with a focus on asthma and chronic obstructive pulmonary disease	29.6%	<£3.0m
Syntopix Group plc	Dermatology antibiotics drug screening and development	17.8%	<£1.0m
Theragenetics Limited	Personalised medicine	25.0%	<£3.0m
Tissue Regenix Limited	Platform technologies for producing highly biocompatible, regenerative tissue implants	27.6%	<£3.0m
Tracsis plc	Crew scheduling software for transportation industry	20.9%	<£3.0m

Company name	Description of business	Group Stake 30 Jun 2008	Fair value of holding 30 June 2008
Wireless Biodevices Limited	Wireless biosensors – first application is blood sensor for colon cancer diagnosis	35.4%	<£0.5m
Xanic Limited	Superior InP components for applications including wireless communication, imaging, radar and security scanners	14.8%	<£0.5m
Xeros Limited	Solvent free dry cleaning and "waterless" washing machines	41.3%	<£0.5m

Table 7: companies created by IP Group Plc

There are 20 incubator stage companies with a fair value of £1.2 million. Those with a value less than £3 million amount to over 40 companies, having a fair value of about £32 million, while the 10 spin-outs valued at more than £3 million each are valued at £115 million in total. Table 8 gives more information about these latter companies.

Company name	Description	Quoted/ Unquoted	Company value 30 Jun 08 £m	Group Stake 30 Jun 08 %	Fair Value of Group holding at:	
					30 June 08 £m	31 Dec 07 £m
Avacta Group plc	Advanced molecular detection and analysis technologies for the biopharmaceutical, homeland security, defence and medical diagnostics industries	Quoted	30.9	23.9%	7.4	6.9
Green Chemicals plc	Environmentally friendly textile and bleaching chemicals	Quoted	30.8	24.5%	7.7	7.5
iQur Limited	Diagnosis and treatment of liver disorders	Unquoted	23.3	17.7%	4.1	4.1

Company name	Description	Quoted/ Unquoted	Company value	Group Stake	Fair Value of Group holding at:	
			30 Jun 08 £m	30 Jun 08 %	30 Jun 08 £m	31 Dec 07 £m
Ilika Technologies Limited	Development and application of high throughput, combinatorial R&D techniques for the discovery of new materials	Unquoted	29.5	23.6%	7.0	7.0
Modern Water plc	Water technologies to address problems of the availability of freshwater and the treatment and disposal of wastewater	Quoted	60.0	23.0%	13.8	12.2
Oxford Advanced Surfaces Group plc	Development and commercialisation of technology enabling modification of the surface properties of materials	Quoted	149.5	15.7%	23.5	12.0
Oxford Catalysts Group plc	Speciality catalysts for the generation of clean fuels, from conventional fossil fuels and renewable sources such as biomass	Quoted	66.9	16.7%	11.2	9.7
Proximagen Neuroscience plc	Developing drugs for the treatment of neurodegenerative diseases	Quoted	20.1	23.5%	4.7	5.4
Photopharmica (Holdings) Limited	Develops novel photosensitisers as products for medical use & has opened up new applications of topical photodynamic therapy	Unquoted	26.0	49.9%	13.0	13.0
Revolymer Limited	Designs, develops and formulates novel polymers that revolutionise consumer products. First application is removable "Clean Gum".	Unquoted	26.3	11.2%	3.0	0.7

Table 8: Spin-outs valued at more than £3 million

The range of sectors covered by these spin-outs is given in Table 9, which serves to emphasise just how broadly based the portfolio has become.

Portfolio analysis – by sector

The Group focuses on five key sectors. An analysis of the portfolio by these sectors is as follows:

Sector	As at 30 Jun 2008			
	Fair Value		Number	
	£m	%	£m	%
Chemicals & Materials	46.7	31%	19	26%
Energy & Renewables	29.0	20%	8	11%
Healthcare & Life Sciences: Non Therapeutics	36.7	25%	21	28%
Healthcare & Life Sciences: Therapeutics	30.3	20%	12	16%
IT & Communications	5.7	4%	14	19%
Total	148.4	100%	74	100%

Table 9: The sector spread of companies

The "Modern" Businesses

The model has worked very well, but there is a limit to the number of university partnerships which can be handled effectively, so a variant has been developed: the so-called "modern" businesses, the name being derived from the chess opening favoured by Dave Norwood. In this case IP Group has researched and then decided upon areas or topics where there is a need for a business, sourced top-level management and then sought out specific intellectual property in universities to provide the scientific basis.

Three such companies now exist:

1. Modern Biosciences is a drug development company that resources late-stage discovery projects from academics and other spin-out companies, conducts early proof of principle   clinical   studies and subsequently out-licences the resulting programmes to the pharmaceutical and biotechnology industries. They have agreements with the Universities of Aberdeen, Dundee, Manchester and Bradford.

2. In a similar way, Modern Water was established to build and exploit a portfolio of water technologies to address problems of the availability of freshwater and the treatment and disposal of waste water. The company was floated on AIM in 2007, and is currently valued at £53 million.

3. Modern Waste has a focus on technologies that improve the economics of waste and recycling with the intention of developing novel technologies into profitable businesses. It is a subsidiary of IP Group.

IP Group has grown to become a substantial business. Highlights of the 2007 Annual Report show that the value of its portfolio was £126 million, an increase in one year of 44%. Cash from sales of equity investments during that year was £8 million, an increase of 158%, while net assets rose to £214 million. Over £30 million was raised by portfolio companies in private funding rounds, with a similar sum being invested.

In all spin-out companies three aspects are vital: the scientific idea or technology, funding and management. There is no shortage of science. Funding ability is cyclical but is normally possible for the really convincing idea. The biggest bottleneck is finding suitable management, company chairmen and non-executive directors.

8

Conclusions

There is no doubt that the exploitation of university generated intellectual property is important. One only has to look at the computing industry and at the world of biotechnology to see that many of the advanced companies have their origins in university laboratories. Not only is this exploitation important, it is also growing and supported by governments across the globe.

The universities themselves welcome the income generated from spin-outs and licensing deals, while individual academic scientists see that activity in this domain can generate improved facilities and funding for students. It is however very important for the universities to remember that their principal roles are teaching and research. Commercial opportunities are a welcome by-product and should come at the end of the research process. We have to be very vigilant to avoid redirecting research and to prevent a distorting of the prime mission. There are dangers.

The Dangers

The essence of universities is that they are open and knowledge is freely disseminated. How does this sit with protecting and exploiting intellectual property? The answer is that there is some discomfort, but workable compromises have emerged. When research is funded by industrial corporations, most academic institutions will agree to short delays in publication so as to protect inventions, and the same thing is found to work when the intellectual property belongs to the university. These delays must not extend beyond a period of months and thesis examinations should not be distorted by commercial considerations. Research students must be protected from exploitation and access to some form of conflicts of interest scrutiny is essential.

It is often helpful for the early stage of a start-up to be housed within a university department, but as soon as possible it is wise to seek external premises. Similarly the role of the academic must be clarified and in general he or she should not be an employee of the company, but rather a technical advisor or non-executive director. Even the latter may become inappropriate as the company grows.

Many of the dangers are subtle. Academics rightly want to research on questions that interest them. Institutions need to be aware when recruiting new staff of the dangers of hiring faculty because their research looks particularly marketable. There are those who take an absolute view that universities and commercial considerations do not mix – that money is the root of all evil. In the modern world such attitudes are not sustainable, but it is equally foolish to be blind to the possible conflicts. Most academic institutions have a "conflicts of interest committee" for this very reason, and it can rule in difficult cases.

The Science For Spin-Outs

Experience has shown that most of the really successful spin-outs have been based on research that was not seen originally to be a likely source of profitable intellectual property. The so-called "blue skies" research is a far better source than that which appears obviously exploitable for profit at the outset. In my own case, when we started working on the application of quantum mechanics to biological molecules, the research seemed esoteric and even dotty rather than commercially orientated. Who would have dreamed that the World Wide Web should have emerged from a particle physics environment?

Of all the prerequisites for successful spin-outs, the easiest to satisfy is that of suitable science. There is so much good research in all countries that is capable of exploitation. All that is required is someone who can recognise the potential. Best of all, this person is the individual who is doing the research and then only needs advice from someone with an understanding of the commercial process, probably the technology transfer professionals.

Management

In much shorter supply are the potential CEOs for the new venture. Here there exists the classic chicken and egg situation. If there have been a lot of spin-outs, management is easier to find. One of the reasons for the great success of spin-outs in California is that there are a lot of people who have done it before. There has been sufficient activity for individuals to recognise that they are the ideal people to get a small company off the ground and possibly to leave when that has been achieved and to repeat the process. The USA has an admirable view of people who have tried and failed. They are not damned for all time, but rather are seen as people who have learned valuable lessons so that they will not repeat old mistakes.

For countries that do not possess the pool of experienced start-up executives life is more difficult. One source of personnel that is expanding is folk from major companies, particularly in the pharmaceutical area, which are restructuring and shedding staff. Such people have the advantage of having good contacts with big companies that can help sales and joint projects, but they have to learn very quickly how to operate in a small team where they have to do their own photocopying and make their own coffee.

Such is the vibrancy of the world of spin-out companies that business schools are increasingly training potential CEOs and giving courses in entrepreneurship. Science graduate students and post-doctoral researchers are more and more showing a preference for working in a spin-out rather than a major company. The latter have had a lot of bad publicity and the young researchers can increasingly see how some of the people in start-up companies have grown rich as well as being able to live and work in desirable surroundings, often close to the universities where they retain friends and useful contacts. Happily, cooperation between business schools and science departments is on the increase – business schools are providing more courses that instil science graduates with basic commercial skills, enabling them to become suitable as executives in spin-outs.

Funding

In addition to some good exploitable science and management the new spin-out will require funds, probably less than typical venture capital organisations like to consider. As discussed earlier, business angels, family and the few specialist sponsors are the main sources, although the growth of university funds is a notable feature, often in part from governmental sources.

As in most commercial activity the availability of funding is cyclical. There have been periods when money is easy to get and people were fighting to be able to invest. Currently we are at the opposite end of the cycle. Venture capital funds that did consider start-ups have withdrawn and in particular the areas of drug discovery and biotechnology are struggling. For the past few years the Alternative Investment Market, AIM, was not only an avenue for exits, but also very newly formed companies were floated. It was possible to have an IPO of a company long before it became profitable and in so doing raise sufficient cash to see the company through several years. At present there is little activity on AIM and the other markers for small companies. Times are hard, but this does provide real opportunities for wise entrepreneurs. Anyone with cash to invest can find some real gems and also take-over some of the companies that are struggling to find second or third round funding. Such entrepreneurs are also starting to amalgamate some of the spin-outs in specific areas to form larger more viable units. As always, times that are difficult for some provide opportunities for others.

The Global University IP Industry

Since it seems most helpful to base this book round a single case study, the emphasis has inevitably been on the situation in the UK. That experience should translate to any other country though, since the essentials are universal. What is more the activity, as with so much in commercial life, is becoming global. The companies which specialise in supporting spin-outs are becoming ever more multinational, with arrangements involving universities in several countries, particularly those where the ownership of intellectual property is clear-cut. There are obvious advantages in involving several countries in any spin-out, notably future sales and tax regimes. In the past the most successful spin-outs have originated in the US, with the UK perhaps the second most fruitful source. Continental Europe is catching up and keen interest is being shown in China and India. I have given lectures on the topic in Japan, Brazil, South Africa and Singapore, and these countries too are eager to embrace the concept. Just as companies look to the Middle East for funds, the rulers of those countries are conscious of the opportunities to foster spin-outs in their own countries as a way of reducing future dependency on oil, but also as a way of exploiting the wasted resources – such as the burning off of low molecular weight hydrocarbons, to say nothing about future needs such as desalination. Science is a universal subject and so too is the exploitation of research for the common benefit of humanity and the welfare of our planet.

People

The universal truth that in the end all endeavours reduce to the skills of the people involved is as applicable to spin-out companies and the exploitation of university generated intellectual property as to all other activities.

The formation of spin-outs demands the interaction of three different groups and has been described as working in a three-dimensional space where the three orthogonal axes are:

1. The academic axis where the researcher wants to fund his or her research.

2. The commercial axis where the intention is to turn the research into products or services.

3. The financial axis where backers want to generate cash.

Spin-out companies, in their creation, require all three and ideally involve individuals who are at least sensitive to the other two axes apart from their own. In the end all these activities come down to people. The short account given in this book has in a sense highlighted three people who have proved to be sufficiently adept at understanding all the aspects. Tim Cook has brought clarity to university technology transfer, Tony Marchington epitomised the type of management required for the start-up and David Norwood had the financial skills to provide funding.

All those qualities are essential ingredients but, from one who has also been involved in this type of activity for many years, it must also be added that creating spin-out companies can be not only hard work and profitable – it can be fun too.

Appendices

Appendix A:
University contact details

United Kindgom

Directory
🖥 www.universitiesuk.ac.uk

Queen Mary, University of London
✉ University of London
Mile End Road
London
E1 4NS
☎ 020 7882 5555
🖥 www.qmul.ac.uk

University of Aberdeen
✉ King's College
Aberdeen
AB24 3FX
☎ 01224 272000
🖥 www.abdn.ac.uk

University of Bath
✉ Bath
BA2 7AY
☎ 01225 388388
🖥 www.bath.ac.uk

University of Bradford
✉ Bradford
West Yorkshire
BD7 1DP
☎ 01274 232323
🖥 www.brad.ac.uk

University of Bristol
✉ Senate House
Tyndall Avenue
Bristol
BS8 1TH
☎ 0117 928 9000
🖥 www.bristol.ac.uk

University of Cambridge
✉ The Old Schools
Trinity Lane
Cambridge
CB2 1TN
☎ 01223 337733
🖥 www.cam.ac.uk

University of Dundee
✉ Nethergate
Dundee
DD1 4HN
☎ 01382 383 000
🖥 www.dundee.ac.uk
@ university@dundee.ac.uk

University of Edinburgh
✉ Old College
South Bridge
Edinburgh
EH8 9YL
☎ 0131 650 1000
Fax 0131 650 2147
🖥 www.ed.ac.uk
@ communications.office@ed.ac.uk

University of Glasgow
✉ University Avenue
Glasgow
G12 8QQ
☎ 0141 330 2000
💻 www.glasgow.ac.uk

University of Leeds
✉ Leeds
LS2 9JT
☎ 0113 243 1751
Fax 0113 244 3923
💻 www.leeds.ac.uk
@ enquiry@leeds.ac.uk

University of Manchester
✉ Oxford Road
Manchester
M13 9PL
☎ 0161 306 6000
💻 www.manchester.ac.uk

University College London
✉ Gower Street
London
WC1E 6BT
☎ 020 7679 2000
💻 www.ucl.ac.uk

University of Oxford
✉ University Offices
Wellington Square
Oxford
OX1 2JD
☎ 01865 270000
💻 www.ox.ac.uk

University of Sheffield
✉ Western Bank
Sheffield
S10 2TN
☎ 0114 222 2000
🖳 www.shef.ac.uk

University of Southampton
✉ University Road
Southampton
SO17 1BJ
☎ 023 8059 5000
Fax 023 8059 3939
🖳 www.soton.ac.uk

University of Surrey
✉ Guildford
Surrey
GU2 7XH
☎ 01483 300800
Fax 01483 300803
🖳 www.surrey.ac.uk

University of Wales
✉ University Registry
King Edward VII Ave
Cardiff
CF10 3NS
☎ 029 2037 6999
🖳 www.wales.ac.uk

University of York
✉ Heslington
York
YO10 5DD
☎ 01904 430000
Fax 01904 433433
🖳 www.york.ac.uk

United States of America

Directory
🖥️ www.stateuniversity.com

Harvard University
✉️ Faculty of Arts and Sciences
University Hall
Cambridge
MA 02138
☎️ 617 495 1000
🖥️ www.harvard.edu

Massachusetts Institute of Technology
✉️ 77 Massachusetts Avenue
Cambridge
MA 02139-4307
☎️ 617 253 1000
🖥️ web.mit.edu

Stanford University
✉️ 450 Serra Mall
Stanford
CA 94305
☎️ 650 723 2300
🖥️ www.stanford.edu

University of California
🖥️ www.universityofcalifornia.edu
Various campuses at Berkeley, Davis, Irvine, Los Angeles, Merced, Riverside, San Diego, San Francisco, Santa Barbara and Santa Cruz.

European Union

Directory
💻 www.eua.be/members-directory

University of Erlangen-Nürnberg
✉ Schlossplatz 4
91054 Erlangen
Germany
☎ +49 9131 85-0
Fax +49 9131 85-22131
💻 www.uni-erlangen.org

Appendix B:
Contacts For Business Start-ups

United Kingdom

Angels Den
Connecting investors and enterpreneurs
☎ 0800 231 6331
🖳 www.angelsden.co.uk
@ wings@angelsden.com

Angel Investment Network
✉ 238 St Margaret's Road
Twickenham
Middlesex
TW1 1NL
🖳 www.angelinvestmentnetwork.co.uk

Business Angel Capital
Linking investors with business people
🖳 www.bacapital.co.uk

British Business Angels Association (BBAA)
Trade association for the early stage investment market, useful
information for investors and entrepreneurs
✉ New City Court
20 St Thomas Street
London
SE1 9RS
☎ 0207 089 2305
🖳 www.bbaa.org.uk
@ info@bbaa.org.uk

Knowledge Transfer Partnerships
Providing knowledge, technology and skills to new businesses

✉ KTP Programme Office AEA
Didcot
Oxfordshire
OX11 0QJ

☎ 0870 190 2829

💻 www.ktponline.org.uk

@ ktp-help@ktponline.org.uk

Library House, Cambridge
A service for investors looking to fund spin-out companies, academics wising to get financial backing for their spin-out company and for corporations looking to merge with or acquire other companies.

✉ The Library House Ltd
4th Floor, Kett House
Station Road
Cambridge
CB1 2JX

☎ 01223 500 550

Fax 01223 472 716

💻 www.libraryhouse.net

@ info@libraryhouse.net

London Business Angels
Investing in new business

✉ GLE Growth Capital
New City Court
20 St Thomas Street
London
SE1 9RS

☎ 0207 089 2303

💻 www.lbangels.co.uk

London Seed Capital
Venture capital fund
✉ New City Court
20 St Thomas Street
London
SE1 9RS
☎ 0207 403 0300
💻 www.gle.co.uk

Oxford Capital Partners
Venture capital firm
✉ Oxford Capital Partners Limited
201 Cumnor Hill
Oxford
OX2 9PJ
☎ 01865 860760
💻 www.oxcp.com

Regional Development Agencies
Helping new UK businesses to compete in regional, and world, markets
✉ Contact details vary by region
💻 www.englandsrdas.com

Wyvern Seed Fund
Support for the early stage commercialisation of research generated by the Universities of Bristol and Southampton
✉ 1 Widcombe Crescent
Bath
BA2 6AH
☎ 01225 472953
💻 www.wyvernfund.com

European Union

Enterprise Ireland
Knowledge and financial support for commercialising research
✉ The Plaza
East Point Business Park
Dublin 3
☎ +(353 1) 727 2000
💻 www.enterprise-ireland.com

United Sates of America

Gaebler Ventures
Resources for entrepreneurs – list of angel investment
companies by US State
✉ Gaebler Ventures
156 N. Jefferson Street
Suite 301
Chicago
IL 60661
💻 www.gaebler.com

Appendix C:
Contacts For Investors

United Kingdom
British Business Angels Association
See Appendix 2: Contacts For Business Start-ups

Europe
European Business Angel Network (EBAN)
Representing European investors' interests
⊠ 3 Rue Abbé Cuypers
1040 Brussels
Belgium
☎ +32 (0) 2 741 24 70
💻 www.eban.org

Canada
National Angel Capital Organization
Representing Canadian investor's interests
⊠ 257 Adelaide Street West, 6th Floor
Toronto
Ontario
M5H 1X9
☎ 416 581 0009
💻 www.angelinvestor.ca

United States of America
Angel Capital Association
⊠ 8527 Bluejacket Street
Lenexa
KS 66214
☎ 913 894 4700
💻 www.angelcapitalassociation.org

Angel Investor News

Internet resources for private investors

www.angel-investor-news.com

Appendix D:
Lawyers, Solicitors And Accountants

Addleshaw Goddard
✉ 150 Aldersgate Street
London
EC1A 4EJ
☎ 020 7606 8855
FAX 020 7606 4390
🖥 www.addleshawgoddard.com

KPMG
✉ 8 Salisbury Square
London
EC4Y 8BB
☎ 020 7311 1000
FAX 020 7311 3311
🖥 www.kpmg.co.uk

Norton Rose LLP
Worldwide locations
United Kingdom contact details:
✉ 3 More London Riverside
London
SE1 2AQ
☎ 020 7283 6000
FAX 020 7283 6500
🖥 www.www.nortonrose.com

Directory
Unico
Representing the technology exploitation companies of UK
universities – directory of legal and accounting firms
🖥 www.unico.org.uk/mcorpaf.htm

Appendix E:
Suggested Further Reading

The Art and Science of Technology Transfer: Moving Technology Out of the Lab and Into Markets by Phyllis L. Speser
(John Wiley & Sons, 2006)

The Ernst and Young Guide to the IPO Value Journey by Ernst and Young
(John Wiley & Sons, 1999)

Initial Public Offerings by Richard Kleeburg
(South Western Educational Publishing, 2004)

Intellectual Property Law by Lionel Bently and Brad Sherman
(OUP Oxford; 3rd edition, 2008)

IPOs and Equity Offerings (Securities Institute Global Capital Markets) by Ross Geddes
(Butterworth-Heinemann, 2003)

The IPO Decision: Why and How Companies Go Public
by Jason Draho
(Edward Elgar Publishing Ltd, 2005)

Start-up: A Practical Guide to Starting and Running a New Business by Tom Harris
(Springer, 2006)

Startup to IPO by Donald H. MacAdam
(Xlibris Corporation, 2004)

Strategic Management of Technology Transfer: The New Challenge on Campus by James Cunningham and Brian Harney
(Oak Tree Press, 2006)

Technology Transfer: Making the Most of Your Intellectual Property
by Neil F. Sullivan
(Cambridge University Press, 2008)

Universities and Intellectual Property: Ownership and Exploitation by
Ann Louise Monotti and Sam Ricketson
(OUP Oxford, 2003)

Index

A

Aberdeen, University of, see universities
Abraham, Sir Edward 17
academics
> benefits for, through being involved in a spin-out 18-19, 43-44, 64
> role of, in a spin-out vi, 11, 18, 37, 41-2, 105, 114

accountants 39, 45-6, 68, 76, 88
> KPMG Peat Marwick 74, 79

Advent 61-62, 66, 67
AIM, see Alternative Investment Market
Alternative Investment Market 122, 123, 125, 133, 140
Amaethon Ltd 123, 126
Amoco 95, 96, 97
angel investors 21, 25, 42, 113, 140
Angle 125
ASSIST 71
Aubrey, Alan 124
Audley, Diana 89

B

Babbage 13
Bailey, Paul
> at Advent 61, 63
> at Barings 67, 77, 83, 94

banks 22, 23, 39, 45, 57, 73, 74, 96, 102, 115, 116
> Barclays Bank 71, 73, 94

Baring Brothers Hambrecht and Quist, see venture capital
Bartlett, Jonathan 91
Barltrop, John 55, 57
Bath, University of 70, 79, 126
Bayh-Dole Act 11-12
Bayley, Hagan 122
BBC 13
Beeson Gregory Ltd vi, 4, 113, 114-127, 122, 123
> Beeson, Andrew 116

C

D

H

I

J

K

P

Q

R

S

T

V

W